The U.S.
Air Force
and Military Careers

by *Wilson Camelo*

Enslow Publishers, Inc.
40 Industrial Road
Box 398
Berkeley Heights, NJ 07922
USA

http://www.enslow.com

c.1

Library of Congress Cataloging-in-Publication Data

Camelo, Wilson.
    The U.S. Air Force and military careers / Wilson Camelo
      p. cm. – (The U.S. Armed Forces and military careers)
    Includes bibliographical references and index.
    ISBN 0-7660-2524-1
    1. United States. Air Force—Juvenile literature. 2. United States. Air Force—
Vocational guidance—Juvenile literature. I. Title. II. Series.
UG633.C1494 2006
358.400973—dc22

                                             2005037882

Printed in the United States of America

10 9 8 7 6 5 4 3 2 1

To Our Readers: We have done our best to make sure all Internet Addresses in this book
were active and appropriate when we went to press. However, the author and the publisher
have no control over and assume no liability for the material available on those Internet
sites or on other Web sites they may link to. Any comments or suggestions can be sent by
e-mail to comments@enslow.com or to the address on the back cover.

Illustration Credits: Department of Defense photo by Rudi Williams, p. 65; Library
of Congress, p. 111 (top); NASA, p. 60; U.S. Air Force graphic, pp. 26, 48, 81, 82, 91,
113 (top); U.S. Air Force photo, pp. 6, 8, 10, 13, 14, 16, 19, 23, 27, 36, 51, 58, 59, 62,
104, 106, 107, 110, 111 (middle and bottom), 112, 113 (middle and bottom), 122 (top),
123; U.S. Air Force photo by 1st Lt. Ellen Harr, p. 54; U.S. Air Force photo by Airman
1st Class Veronica Pierce, p. 109; U.S. Air Force photo by Anna Risse, p. 85; U.S. Air
Force photo by Danny Meyer, p. 88; U.S. Air Force photo by Larry Davenport, p. 72;
U.S. Air Force photo by Master Sgt. Efrain Gonzalez, pp. 73, 76; U.S. Air Force photo
by Master Sgt. Jeff Bohn, p. 71; U.S. Air Force photo by Master Sgt. Val Gempis,
p. 97; U.S. Air Force photo by Robbin Creswell, p. 86; U.S. Air Force photo by
Samantha Housman, p. 70; U.S. Air Force photo by Senior Airman Brian Ferguson,
p. 63; U.S. Air Force Photo by Senior Airman Matthew Rosine, pp. 33, 122 (bottom);
U.S. Air Force photo by Senior Airman Mike Meares, p. 79; U.S. Air Force photo by
Senior Airman Neal X. Joiner, p. 4; U.S. Air Force photo by Senior Master Sgt. Elaine
Mayo, pp. 3, 41; U.S. Air Force photo by Staff Sgt. Ken Bergmann, pp. 1, 30–31; U.S.
Air Force photo by Staff Sgt. Michael R. Holzworth, pp. 2 (right), 39; U.S. Air Force
photo by Staff Sergeant Willaim Greer, p. 43; U.S. Air Force photo by Tech. Sgt. Ben
Bloker, pp. 2 (center), 99; U.S. Air Force photo by Tech. Sgt. Scott Reed, p. 37; U.S. Air
Force Photo by Tech. Sgt. Scott T. Sturkol, pp. 2 (left), 95.

Cover Illustration: U.S. Air Force photo by Tech. Sgt. Ben Bloker (front cover);
Wilson Camelo (back cover).

Contents

▲ President Bush leaves Air Force One after returning to Andrews Air Force Base on September 11, 2001.

One

A New Air Force Emerges

When Air Force One took off from Andrews Air Force Base in Maryland on September 10, 2001, no one knew how different the mission of bringing President George W. Bush to Florida would turn out. Actually, when Air Force One returned to Andrews on September 11, a new era for the U.S. Air Force would begin.

Bush was in Florida to talk to children about reading and education. On his way to an elementary school around 9 A.M. he learned that a plane had crashed into one of the "twin towers" of the World Trade Center (WTC). Most assumed it was an accident. However, soon a second plane crashed into the other tower.[1] Terrorists had struck, and the U.S. Air Force sprang into action.

By 9:45 A.M., Bush was on board Air Force One and using the Air Force's secure communications to speak with Vice President Dick Cheney at the White House. There was much confusion in the

Staff Sergeant Andy Brunn

Staff Sergeant Andrew Brunn was a member of the New York Air Guard at Stewart Air Base and a firefighter with a New York Fire Department in Lower Manhattan. Brunn completed fire academy training in July 2001, and only two months later he was one of the first responders to the attacks in New York City. Brunn was killed while climbing the stairwell in the WTC north tower. He is believed to have reached the thirty-seventh floor when the tower collapsed. "No one knows the thoughts of firefighter Andrew 'Andy' Brunn as he sped toward the burning World Trade Center," wrote Sergeant Patricia Pullar, public affairs officer at Stewart. "We only know he wanted to help save as many lives as possible."[2]

early hours of the attack as to how many hijacked planes were still in the air or if Air Force One was a target.

The president authorized the military to shoot down any civilian aircraft that was a threat. The staff at First Air Force (1st AF) at Tyndall Air Force Base in Florida began coordinating the aerial response with the North American Aerospace Defense Command (NORAD) at Peterson Air Force Base, Colorado. Together, 1st AF and NORAD are responsible for patrolling and defending American airspace.

Air Force fighter jets, such as F-15s from Langley Air Force Base in Virginia, were soon streaking across the sky responding to the attacks. One headed toward a hijacked aircraft thought to be targeting Washington, D.C. However, before the F-15 arrived, the plane crashed in western Pennsylvania after passengers fought back for control of the aircraft. Other jet fighters were sent to provide air cover, called Combat Air Patrols, over cities like New York and Washington, D.C.

Even more Air Force aircraft and units also responded to the attacks. A C-5 cargo aircraft from Westover Air Reserve Base in Massachusetts, on its way to Australia, was rerouted to Travis Air Force Base in California to pick up a search-and-rescue unit and bring its members to New York City to search the World Trade Center rubble for survivors.

While the public does not know all its specific protective capabilities, Air Force One has many defensive systems. However, rather than take risks, when Air Force One took off from Florida, it flew at a very high altitude where it had a better chance of outrunning a civilian airliner.[3] Air Force crews took Bush to Barksdale Air Force Base in Louisiana. There, he made several phone calls from a conference room to Vice President Cheney, Defense Secretary Donald Rumsfeld, and New York senator Charles Schumer. At the base, President Bush made a speech, assuring America that security measures are being taken.[4]

Air Force One then left Barksdale and went to Offutt Air Force Base in Nebraska. The president and staff went to the base's command post deep underground. After a one-hour meeting, Bush reboarded Air Force One. With F-16 fighter aircraft flying protective cover, he returned to Andrews Air Force Base where he boarded a helicopter to the White House. As he approached the White House, the president could see the Pentagon, which also had

▲ Air Force One is pictured flying over Mount Rushmore.

been hit by a hijacked civilian airliner that day. "The mightiest building in the world is on fire," he said.[5]

From that day on, the Air Force would change. It would have a more direct role in defending the homeland from aerial attack in the War on Terrorism. However, the Air Force would need a different mentality to respond to the battles it would face in the twenty-first century. The enemy would no longer directly challenge the Air Force in the air: it would be nimbler, using terrorist tactics and blending into society.

Two

History of American Aviation

Flying in strong winds over the North Carolina coast on December 17, 1903, bicycle makers Wilbur and Orville Wright became the first humans to achieve controlled, powered flight.

The Wright brothers were not the first to fly a heavier-than-air craft. For more than a century, people had flown in balloons and gliders. The problem was not getting in the air; it was getting in the air when one wanted and steering and landing safely.[1]

In 1908, the U.S. Army invested in a steerable airship, called a dirigible, which could stay in the air for two hours and fly at a rate of 20 miles per hour.[2] Later that year, Orville Wright piloted a plane during a demonstration for Army authorities. Unfortunately, the plane crashed, killing a signal corpsman, Lieutenant Thomas Selfridge. He was the first U.S. military aviation casualty.[3]

However, many in the United States did not recognize the military use for airplanes, so the

Wright brothers went to Europe to promote their accomplishment. British, French, German, and Italian military forces quickly adopted aircraft into their arsenals.

The U.S. Army finally purchased its first airplane from the Wright brothers in 1909.[4] The Wright

▲ After the Wright brothers' first successful flight, Orville Wright made several more flights. Here, his plane soars above Fort Myers, Florida, on September 9, 1908.

brothers trained the first military pilots. Even though they successfully used rifles and bombs to shoot targets from a plane, the Army did not think aircraft could do more than reconnaissance, or checking on the enemy's position. In 1912, the Army announced it would no longer fund aviation experiments.

As a result, airplanes were not used in combat until 1916 when General John Pershing led an unsuccessful mission to find and capture Mexican revolutionary Pancho Villa. But war was ravaging much of Europe, and aviation would play an important role on the continent.

World War I

The "war to end all wars" had been fought for almost three years when the United States entered it in April 1917. American aviation forces had only 131 officers, of whom just 26 were considered fully trained. There were no combat aircraft, no units trained in warfare, and no pilots with combat experience. European pilots already had three years' experience.[5]

The United States had no plans to build an air service that could fight in Europe or any capabilities to quickly build fighter aircraft. In the year before America entered the war, civilian factories had only delivered 64 of the 366 planes ordered. On May 24, 1917, President Woodrow Wilson received a telegram from French Premier Alexandre Ribot requesting that America send 4,500 planes and

5,000 pilots to the front by spring 1918. The request helped start the Army's aviation expansion.[6]

In Europe, American pilots trained with their Allied partners and flew reconnaissance missions in the fall of 1918. On the morning of October 5, 1918, the 50th Aero Squadron observation unit was on a mission to find and bring supplies to three battalions of the 77th Division. Flying low in fog and hostile fire, the unit went searching for a missing battalion. They dropped supplies where they thought the battalion was, but the supplies were gathered up by the Germans.[7]

The next morning, Lieutenants Harold Goettler and Erwin Bleckley took off in their DH-4 aircraft to continue searching. They returned to where they thought the battalion was located, but came under attack. The lieutenants flew back to the airfield for repairs and returned again to the area, but German gunners were waiting. Goettler and Bleckley were attacked and were shot down and killed. They were later awarded the Medal of Honor. The day after the pilots were killed, survivors of the "Lost Battalion," as they came to be known, were located.[8]

Perhaps the best-known American World War I era aviation commander was General William "Billy" Mitchell. Concerned that inexperienced units were being sent into combat, Mitchell took control of training the First Army Air Service. He soon had under his control the largest group of air forces ever assembled in a single operation during World War I. Mitchell's 1,481 aircraft and 30,000 men came from

American, French, Italian and
British forces and were likely
the first aerial coalition.[9]

The First Army Air
Service's first battle took
place from September 12 to
September 16 with impres-
sive results. American pilots
made thirty-three hundred
flights over enemy lines,
fired thirty thousand rounds,

▲ General William "Billy" Mitchell is
pictured in his early years as a pilot.

made more than one thousand bomb attacks
destroying twelve enemy balloons and sixty
planes.[10] The battle also produced the first two
American aces (pilots who down more than five
enemy aircraft), Captain Eddie Rickenbacker and
Second Lieutenant Frank Luke.

The last American air victory of World War I
occurred on November 10, 1918, when Major
Maxwell Kirby shot down a German Fokker while
flying his Spad-13 on a patrol mission. Kirby
attacked the unsuspecting German from above and
fired his machine gun within fifty feet.[11] The war
ended the next day.

Overall, American aviators were credited with
destroying 776 enemy planes and 72 enemy balloons. They took more than 18,000 photographs and
dropped 275,000 pounds of bombs. They lost 290
planes and 37 balloons. They also had 569 battle
casualties, 164 aviators killed in action, 102 cap-
tured, and 200 missing in action.[12]

▲ Captain Eddie Rickenbacker poses with his plane. Rickenbacker was the American "Ace of Aces" in World War I. Before he became a pilot, he was a race car driver.

After World War I

America learned many lessons about airpower during the First World War, and military commanders soon began to develop ways to fight future air wars. Mitchell returned from Europe ready to play a role in shaping the future of airpower only to discover his position as director of Military Aeronautics was eliminated by Chief of the Air Service, General Charles Menoher. In addition, Congress reduced the Air Service from two hundred thousand people to only ten thousand. General Menoher told manufacturers that "not a dollar is available for the purchase of new aircraft."[13] The aviation budget projected for $83 million was cut to only $25 million; meanwhile, the British increased their spending to $350 million.[14]

Mitchell criticized these actions and believed in the need for a separate air force. He bragged to Congress that he could sink or destroy any Navy ship, and that for the cost of one battleship they could buy one thousand bombers. Congress ordered the Navy to provide Mitchell with old ships he could use in a test. The Navy thought Mitchell would fail. Secretary of the Navy Josephus Daniel said, "I am so confident that neither the Army nor Navy aviators can hit the *Iowa* when she is underway that I would be perfectly willing to be on board her when they bomb her."[15]

In February 1921, Mitchell gathered nearly one thousand men and two hundred fifty airplanes at Langley Field in Virginia to practice. The test came on June 21, using the German battleship *Ostfriesland* as a target ship, which had been turned over to the United States after World War I. The Navy considered the ship "unsinkable." However, in only twenty-two minutes, the planes bombed and sank the *Ostfriesland*. Mitchell earned instant fame around the world.[16]

Mitchell soon went to the Pacific to gather information. He found poor cooperation between the intelligence services. The growth in Japanese industry, and the increase in their air power, concerned him enough to predict that one day the Japanese would attack Pearl Harbor from the air. When he returned to the United States in 1924, he found the Air Service was still in poor shape, and his predictions about Japan were not taken seriously. Mitchell continued

▲ A bomb explodes on a target ship, the *Ostfriesland*, during Billy Mitchell's demonstration of the might of air power on July 21, 1921.

voicing his disagreements with the War Department until President Calvin Coolidge ordered him court-martialed.[17]

The trial lasted seven weeks, but the jury took only forty minutes to find Mitchell guilty on all charges. He was sentenced to a reduced rank and loss of all pay for five years. He retired instead. Mitchell was later vindicated when many of his predictions about airpower came true, including the one about Pearl Harbor.

World War II

By the time Japanese lieutenant Akira Sakamoto dropped the first Japanese bomb on Pearl Harbor on

December 7, 1941, the military role of airpower was well established. At the time of the attack, there were 231 Army Air Force planes in Hawaii. Some were considered fighter aircraft and others, like the B-17, were bombers. However, less than half of the aircraft were considered fully operational.[18]

In fact, it was a flight of B-17s on the way to Oahu early that morning that confused Lieutenant Kermit Tyler, who did not realize the strange "blips" on the radar were Japanese attack aircraft. With the attack, the United States was thrust into World War II in the Pacific. The Japanese continued their aggressive attacks throughout the South Pacific. However, at the time, U.S. aircraft did not have enough range to reach Japan from Hawaii.

In April 1942, the United States would have a small measure of revenge through an innovative air strike on mainland Japan. Lieutenant Colonel Jimmy Doolittle created a plan to launch B-25 bombers from the deck of the Navy carrier *Hornet*. Volunteers were found and only informed they would be flying the most dangerous mission of their lives. Crews trained at Eglin Field in Florida by flying off a patch of airstrip marked with the width and length of the *Hornet*'s deck.[19]

The plan was to launch the B-25s about four hundred miles from the Japanese coast, have them bomb sites in Japan, and then land in either China or Russia. Landing in Japan would have meant an instant execution. Most of the B-25's guns and equipment were removed to make them as light as possible to conserve fuel.

However, on the day of the attack, April 18, 1942, the *Hornet* was spotted by a Japanese boat, and the attack had to take place from 650 miles away.[20] Doolittle led the attack and was the pilot of the first B-25 to take off from the *Hornet*. The B-25s struck Tokyo and other Japanese cities. Many B-25 crews, low on fuel, bailed out, killing one crewman. Only one B-25 landed safely in the Soviet Union. Three aircraft came down in Japanese-occupied China and the crews were later executed. While the damage to Japan was not severe, the attack gave the enemy a jolt and the American people a much-needed morale boost. Doolittle was promoted to brigadier general and later awarded the Medal of Honor.

In Europe, Army Air Force aircraft and personnel were sent to fight with the allies against Germany. Again, bombers would play a significant role in turning the tide and ending the war.

One key to defeating Germany was destroying its military industrial capabilities, like ball-bearing factories. The bombing was highly inaccurate, the weather in Europe

CAREER PROFILE

Frank Medina

Corporal Frank Medina of the Army Air Force was a tail gunner on a B-24 when his aircraft was shot down over Italy. He and the crew parachuted out of the plane and landed in a cornfield. Dodging machine-gun fire, he was trapped behind enemy lines for eight months. He survived by using his military training and assistance from friendly Italians. His story is well documented in his book *Ciao Francesco.*[21]

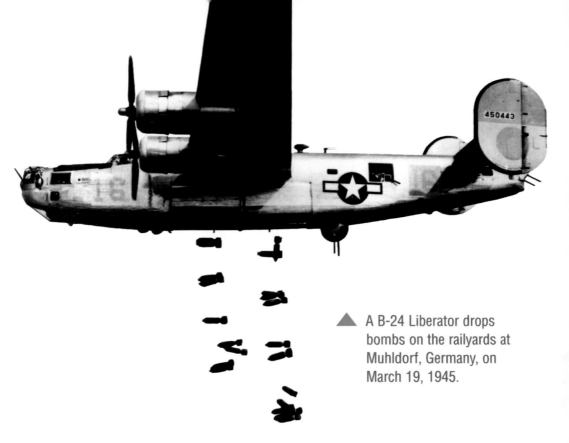

▲ A B-24 Liberator drops bombs on the railyards at Muhldorf, Germany, on March 19, 1945.

was poor, and bombers had to fly to their targets at very high altitudes to avoid antiaircraft artillery. As a result, hundreds of bombers were often needed on a single mission to destroy a target. In addition, fighter escorts did not have enough fuel to escort the bombers all the way to the target. Many bombers were shot down. Morale was low among bomber pilots. The War Department started a policy that allowed bomber crews who successfully flew twenty-five consecutive missions to return home. The first crew to do this was from the *Memphis Belle*, named for a crewmember's girlfriend.

On June 6, 1944, the United States launched the D-day invasion against German forces in Europe. Air forces conducted bombing missions ahead of

American ground troops that were attacking in places like Normandy, France. Fighters provided aerial support for invading troops, cargo aircraft carried critical supplies, and other planes dropped paratroopers behind enemy lines. The end result of the massive invasion was Germany's surrender on May 8, 1945, also called V-E day.

Fighting in the Pacific continued in Japan and other Pacific islands until B-29 bombers dropped atomic bombs on the Japanese cities of Hiroshima and Nagasaki. World War II was over on August 15, 1945, but, not before more than forty thousand Army Air Force members were killed in action and fifteen thousand in training or accidents in the United States.[22]

Three

The Air Force Is Born

The Army Air Force's success in World War II proved to many that airpower no longer belonged under control of the Army. In December 1945, President Harry Truman spoke about developing a separate department for airpower.[1]

The Navy was opposed because they wanted to be solely responsible for protecting the borders of the United States. On September 18, 1947, after the National Security Act was passed, the Air Force was born. W. Stuart Symington became the first secretary of the Air Force, and Carl Spaatz became the first Air Force chief of staff.[2]

The Air Force soon faced a test in Germany. The Soviet Union wanted the Allies to leave a divided Berlin. To counter the Soviets, the Air Force flew thousands of missions to bring aid to the Western half of the city. This massive effort in 1948 was called "The Berlin Airlift."[3]

Korean War

On June 25, 1950, North Korean troops and tanks charged south across the 38th parallel toward Seoul, the capital of the Republic of Korea. War broke out, and the United Nations asked its members to help defend South Korea. Until enough U.S. troops could be deployed in the south, it was the Far Eastern Air Force that largely defended against the aggressors.

The United States had entered the jet era, but it was not the only nation with capable airplanes. The first effective combat jet was the Russian MiG-15.[4] Soon, the Air Force introduced the F-80 Shooting Star and F-86 Sabre to face the Russian fighters in areas known as "MiG Alley," the communist stronghold in northwest Korea.

At first, the Air Force provided defensive support, but on October 7, 1950, President Harry Truman authorized U.S. troops to go after retreating North Korean forces across the 38th parallel. American and South Korean forces entered the North Korean capital of Pyongyang on October 19. Far Eastern Air Force B-29s and B-26s bombed targets in North Korea, while B-26s, F-51s, and F-80s provided close air support to ground troops.[5]

In 1952, the Air Force replaced many of its F-86Es with F-86Fs, which had more powerful engines and improved wing edges that allowed them to better compete with the MiG-15. The Communists restricted their flights to MiG Alley and often avoided aerial combat with F-86 pilots. By August

▲ An F-86 Sabre launches its missiles.

and September, MiG pilots became more aggressive, and aerial engagements occurred almost daily. However, U.S. pilots had the upper hand. For example, from May to June 1953, F-86F forces claimed 165 aerial victories while losing only 3 aircraft.[6]

After two years of negotiations, the Korean War ended on July 27, 1953. More than fifty-four thousand Americans died in the war.[7] The dividing line between North and South Korea remained at the 38th Parallel, where the two sides had battled to a standstill.

Following the Korean War, the United States

entered an arms and space race with the Soviet Union. The Russians were the first to go into space in 1957 when they launched their satellite, *Sputnik*. They were also the first to put a man into space. The United States followed by putting its own manned spacecraft into orbit, and President John F. Kennedy promised to have a man on the moon by 1969. That occurred during the Richard Nixon presidency, almost six years after Kennedy was assassinated. In addition to space exploration, both Russian- and American-made nuclear missiles were developed and deployed throughout Europe. Both sides kept each other in check through a system called Mutually Assured Destruction, or MAD. It meant each side had enough nuclear weapons to destroy the other side, so neither would benefit by striking first.

In 1962, nuclear war seemed possible when Air Force U-2 spy planes flying over Cuba came back with images of Russian missile sites under construction. If completed, the missiles in Cuba could reach the eastern United States. President Kennedy declared Cuba under quarantine, and established an aerial and naval blockade of supplies to Cuba. The world held its breath. Eventually Russian Premier Nikita Khrushchev backed down.

Vietnam War

Vietnam was divided in two in 1954 after the French, who had colonized the country, were defeated. The north, a communist regime, and the south, under an anti-communist leader, soon resumed fighting. In 1961, the United States began training the South Vietnamese armed forces and conducting active operations like reconnaissance.[8]

At the end of 1961, President John F. Kennedy's advisors recommended more American involvement in Vietnam. By 1963, there were fifteen thousand Americans in Vietnam. With Lyndon Johnson as president in 1964, the United States began a bombing campaign. However, American leadership in Washington wanted to control the war in Vietnam so they would not lose American support. Leaders in Washington thought that by "sending signals" to the North Vietnamese through limited bombing they would stop hostilities.

However, the North Vietnamese never believed that Americans had enough commitment to be a threat. Although more bombs were dropped on Vietnam than in all of World War II, much of it was not effective because American political leaders did not want to target civilian areas and encourage negative press coverage. Regulations in warfare, called Rules of Engagement (ROE), were established that restricted what Americans could do. For example, at one point Americans could not strike a surface-to-air missile facility unless an actual missile was installed on the launcher and a missile was shot at an American aircraft.

The United States launched an air campaign called "Rolling Thunder" in 1965, using aircraft like the F-105 and the F-4 Phantom to strike targets over

Airman First Class John L. Levitow

John L. Levitow was a loadmaster on an AC-47 aircraft flying a night mission in Vietnam when it was struck by a mortar round. The explosion ripped a hole through the wing and sent fragments into the fuselage. The whole crew was injured. An explosion tore an activated flare from one crew-member's hand. Levitow, suffering from more than forty fragment wounds, staggered to his feet and saw the smoking flare.

Realizing the plane could catch on fire and crash if the flare ignited inside, Levitow started toward the smoking flare. However, the air-craft was partially out of control so the flare was rolling wildly from side to side and Levitow could not grab it with his hands. Instead, he threw himself on the burning flare. Hugging the flare to his body, he dragged himself to the back of the aircraft and hurled the flare through a cargo door. It ignited safely outside the aircraft. His actions saved the crew from certain death.

cities like Hanoi. The North Vietnamese countered with aircraft like MiG-17s and MiG-21s, but their antiaircraft and surface-to-air missiles were a bigger threat, claiming many U.S. aircraft and crews. In 1966 alone, the Air Force lost 2,257 aircraft.[9]

When Richard Nixon became president in 1969 he continued discussions to end the war. However, he sus-pended peace talks at one point and authorized a major air campaign called Operation Linebacker. It was the most effective use of American air-power in Vietnam because it took out many of the targets that were previously off-limits for political reasons. When peace talks resumed and then failed again, the Americans launched Operation Linebacker II. Fifteen B-52 bombers were lost during the eleven-day offensive, but

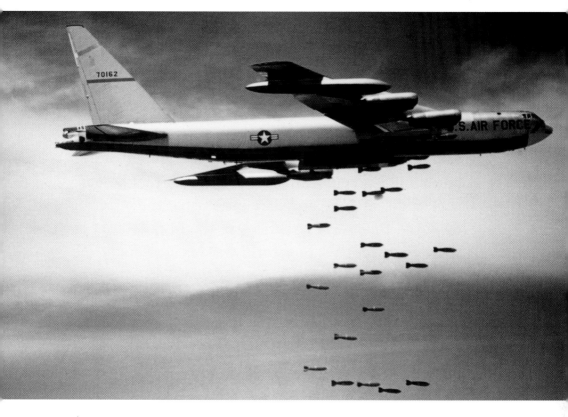

▲ The B-52 Stratofortress was instrumental in the bombing campaign over North Vietnam in the 1960s.

according to some airforce analysts, it proved what airpower could have achieved during the war if properly used. In January 1973, negotiations to end the war restarted, and an agreement was finally signed. Americans headed home by March. Two years later, the communists in the north unified all of Vietnam under their power.[10]

Persian Gulf War

In August 1990, Saddam Hussein's Iraqi military invaded neighboring Kuwait, which is rich with oil and has access to the Persian Gulf. A small group of U.S. Air Force fighter jets were the only defense between Saddam's forces and the oil fields of nearby Saudi Arabia.

The United Nations passed a resolution demanding Saddam leave Kuwait or face serious consequences. When he refused, the United States and its allies began Operation Desert Shield. Soon, thousands of U.S. and foreign troops and aircraft deployed to several countries in the Middle East to show Saddam that the world was serious about his forces leaving Kuwait. They also wanted to prevent Iraq from invading other countries.

The Air Force sent some of its newest weapons including the F-117 stealth fighter. It was considered a stealth aircraft since it was designed to deflect and absorb radar. In addition, a new line of "smart bombs" were introduced. They used satellites, radar, and lasers to guide them to a target.

President George H.W. Bush gave Saddam until January 17, 1991, to remove his forces from Kuwait or face a massive attack. The deadline passed and Operation Desert Shield turned into Operation Desert Storm. A wave of F-117 stealth fighters soon entered Iraqi airspace undetected and bombed numerous targets in the Iraqi capital of Baghdad. Although the F-117 had been used before, the Persian Gulf War was the first time the world saw the capabilities of stealth technology.

Air Force fighter and bomber aircraft began hitting Saddam's power plants, bridges, and communications posts. Saddam's forces were essentially left blind, mute, and deaf. Unable to communicate with his generals and forced to sleep in a different location almost every night, Saddam Hussein saw his military fall apart. Thousands of troops surrendered to coalition forces and what was left of Saddam's air force escaped to Iran.

After weeks of aerial bombing, the ground offensive began. It lasted only one hundred hours. Iraqi forces were driven out of Kuwait and Operation Desert Storm was over.

Kosovo

After his election in 1989, Yugoslav President Slobodan Milosevic imposed Serbian rule in Kosovo, a small province within Serbia. He began a campaign of violence against the ethnic Kosovar Albanians, resulting in the death of more than two hundred fifty thousand civilians by 1995.

In 1998, Milosevic ordered an attack against the Albanian guerrilla force called the Kosovo Liberation Army. Some eighty civilians were killed. The United States sent an ambassador to Belgrade to convince Milosevic to stop targeting civilians. When Milosevic refused, the United Nations passed Security Council Resolution 1199 calling for the end of hostilities. Milosevic initially agreed to let a North Atlantic Treaty Organization (NATO) group into Kosovo to monitor compliance, but he continued his violence against the Albanians. Following other attempts to convince Milosevic to negotiate, and armed with U-2 imagery of mass graves in Kosovo, the United States and NATO gave Milosevic an ultimatum.

He refused to comply and war began. This would be no ordinary war, however. Concerned over lack of congressional and NATO support for a ground war, which could result in many combat casualties, President Bill Clinton called for the conflict to be conducted solely from the air. On March 29, 1999, the first all-air conflict, named Operation Allied Force, was launched.

The first phase of the air campaign was to take out the country's integrated air defense system (IADS) and other targets to show that NATO could attack from the air with minimum collateral, or unintended, damage. The mountainous terrain was challenging for bombing and the weather was usually cloudy. This meant precision-guided munitions (PGMs) would be the weapons of choice. In Desert Storm, 10 percent of the aircraft could deliver PGMs, but during Operation Allied Force that number was 90 percent.[11]

Operation Allied Force marked the combat debut of the B-2 stealth bomber, and the first time the Air Force used its three heavy bombers—the B-2, B-52, and B-1—together in combat. All told, they dropped more than eleven thousand out of the more than twenty-three thousand American bombs during

▼ B-2 stealth bombers were used during Operation Allied Force.

the conflict.[12] B-2s flew nonstop to Kosovo from Whiteman Air Force Base in Missouri on missions that lasted around thirty hours to drop satellite-guided bombs on enemy targets.

Stealth technology suffered its first combat loss. Serb missile operators on the ground knew that an F-117 would enter their area and hit the F-117 with a surface-to-air missile when it briefly became visible on radar as it opened its bomb doors. The pilot ejected and was rescued.[13]

On June 9, 1999, Milosevic accepted a peace agreement to allow fifty thousand NATO-led forces into the country. Operation Allied Force was over. In the end, allied crews flew 38,004 sorties in all, of which more than 23,300 were combat missions.

Four

The War on Terrorism

As the rubble burned following the attacks of September 11, 2001, plans for America's response were under way. President Bush spoke before Congress nine days later:

> And we will pursue nations that provide aid or safe haven to terrorism. Every nation, in every region, now has a decision to make. Either you are with us, or you are with the terrorists. From this day forward, any nation that continues to harbor or support terrorism will be regarded by the United States as a hostile regime.

The United States, he said, would not wait to be attacked. This policy would later become known as the Bush Doctrine. In that same speech, he gave an ultimatum to the Taliban government in Afghanistan, which was protecting the Al-Qaeda terrorist group and its leader Osama Bin Laden, to close terrorist training camps and hand over terrorists.[1]

Al-Qaeda was thought to have been responsible for the September 11 terrorists attacks.

Afghanistan

The Taliban refused. On October 7, 2001, the first military strike in the war on terrorism, called Operation Enduring Freedom, began.[2] On the first night of the conflict, B-2 stealth bombers were launched from Whiteman AFB in Missouri on the longest-distance combat mission in the history of aviation. Six B-2s flew forty-four missions to Afghanistan, dropping satellite-guided bombs and

During Operation Enduring Freedom, Airman 1st Class Cody Braemar mans an M-249 automatic weapon while on guard duty at Karshi-Khanabad Air Base in Uzbekistan.

landing on Diego Garcia, an island controlled by Britain in the Indian Ocean.[3]

In addition to fighting the Taliban, Air Force aircraft were also involved in helping deliver needed food and medicine to the Afghan people. On February 7, 2002, General Tommy Franks, commander of U.S. Central Command (CENTCOM), the group responsible for fighting wars in areas like the Middle East, declared Afghanistan was no longer a safe haven for Al Qaeda. This was due in part to the work of the U.S. Air Force.[4]

While the main conflict was over, much work was left in Afghanistan—finding Bin Laden, rebuilding the country, and preparing for its first democratic elections. Only three years later, 8 million people voted during the historic election on October 9, 2004.[5] They elected Hamid Karzai as their first president.

Iraq

After Afghanistan, President Bush turned his sights on Saddam Hussein and his suspected weapons of mass destruction (WMDs) in Iraq. Since the end of the first Gulf War in 1991, numerous countries and the United Nations called for Saddam to disclose and disarm any WMDs. Saddam had used WMDs in the past. From 1987–88 his forces used poison gas on forty Kurdish villages, killing thousands of civilians. Saddam defied the United Nations (U.N.) and the world. On many occasions since 1991, he had kicked U.N. inspectors out of Iraq or did not provide them all the paperwork to show that he had disposed of his WMDs, as he claimed.

Saddam was given his last opportunity when the U.N. Security Council unanimously passed Resolution 1441 on November 8, 2002. Saddam again refused and the United States and some of its allies decided to attack Iraq, although a majority of U.N. countries did not approve.

On March 17, 2003, President Bush gave Saddam and his sons forty-eight hours to leave Iraq or face a military conflict.[6] Operation Iraqi Freedom began on March 19, 2003. On the opening night of the campaign, the president was told that some "high-value" targets were meeting in a secret compound. President Bush ordered an attack on the location since he thought Saddam Hussein was there. With only two hours' notice, the Air Force sprang into action. Two F-117 stealth fighters dropped bombs on the compound in an effort to take out Saddam and quickly end the war. However, Saddam was not there.

Soon, hundreds of Air Force aircraft—from fighters and bombers to air refuelers, surveillance craft, and helicopters—joined forty-nine coalition countries, organized by President Bush, in taking out Saddam's command and control elements and military targets.

Air Force aircraft like the A-10 and MC-130 flew close air support missions to assist Marine and Army ground forces. By taking out tanks, artillery, radar, and reinforced locations, the Air Force

▲ The 332nd Expeditionary Civil Engineer Squadron detonates an unexploded bomb found during the war in Iraq.

helped to reduce the resistance U.S. ground troops encountered.

Six weeks later, on May 1, 2003, the president said that while much dangerous work was still left to do, major combat operations in Iraq were over.

The Air Force controlled many of the remaining Iraqi airfields and airports, including Baghdad International Airport. Soon, numerous Air Force airplanes were flying in and out of the airport, bringing supplies to the frontline troops. To help ensure that America's largest cargo aircraft, the C-5 Galaxy, could come in with its 270,000 pound capacity loads, the Air Force sent reservists from

Westover Air Reserve Base in Massachusetts to establish an air terminal operations center (ATOC). This ATOC served as a mobile air traffic control operation to ensure the mammoth plane could safely land in Baghdad.

As of 2006, the Air Force was still helping to support ground troops as Americans and Iraqis fought armed insurgents. The Air Force of today will continue to be expected to face these types of challenges.

▲ Seen through a nightvision camera, Staff Sergeant Carl Hill uses a laser to highlight a target to be destroyed, while Technical Sergeant Scott McDaniel talks to an inbound aircraft in the background. The two men are on a mission in Iraq.

The Air Force Today

In the 1990s, the number of airmen in the Air Force was reduced by approximately 30 percent, yet the amount of deployments or missions increased. Air Force members were finding themselves away from home more often to respond to events around the world. Many of these operations required the continuous presence of people and airplanes. For example, after Operation Desert Storm, the United Nations ordered no-fly zones in the northern and southern parts of Iraq to protect civilians. These civilians were being attacked from the air by Saddam Hussein's forces in retaliation for supporting the U.N. coalition. Called Operation Northern Watch and Operation Southern Watch, Air Force F-15 and F-16 fighters patrolled these areas.

However, these types of missions caused a lot of strain on Air Force people and equipment. The Air Force needed a better way to manage its resources while giving battle commanders enough strength to complete missions. Air Force leaders also wanted to find a way to give Air Force troops more notice of when they would deploy and provide time for them to rest and recuperate before their next deployment overseas.

On August 4, 1998, Air Force secretary F. Whitten Peters and Air Force chief of staff General Michael Ryan announced that the Air Force would organize its combat and support assets into ten Aerospace Expeditionary Forces (AEFs).

Each of the AEFs would contain the Air Force weapon systems, people, and command and control needed to complete missions anywhere in the world.

▲ Airmen take part in a field-training exercise at a base in Italy before their upcoming AEF rotation.

AEFs would be "on call" in pairs to respond to world events for a ninety-day period every fifteen months. For example, AEFs 1 and 2 would be on call to deploy if needed from January to March; AEFs 3 and 4 would be on call from April to June, and so on. This cycle would then be repeated every fifteen months. Air Force people and aircraft were assigned to one of the AEFs so they knew exactly when they would be on call to deploy.

The AEF concept became a reality in January 2000. While AEFs helped airmen deal with recurring deployments and small-scale "pop-up" crisis events, the AEF was not designed for fighting a major crisis. If war or a major crisis broke out, all resources would be used.[1] This occurred following the attacks on September 11, 2001, causing the Air Force to temporarily abandon the AEF concept.

The AEF concept resumed in July 2003. However, due to increased needs around the world, Air Force chief of staff General John Jumper extended AEF deployments to 120 days, up from the original 90 days. This meant airmen would be away from home one month longer. However, he also announced that the original fifteen-month rotation cycle would be extended to twenty months, so there was more time between deployments.[2]

Increased Role of the Reserves

Part of what made the AEF concept work was using all available resources, including the Air Force

Reserve (AFR) and Air National Guard (ANG). In 2004, ANG and AFR airmen made up almost 14 percent of the total Air Force population. There were 107,000 ANG and 75,800 AFR troops compared to 359,000 active duty airmen.[3] When factoring in the aircraft and equipment, reserve forces make up about 45 percent of the total Air Force resources. This meant the active duty Air Force needed to use more reserves to fight the war on terrorism. By March 27, 2002, there were 35,981 ANG and AFR airmen called to active duty for one to two years to fight the war on terrorism, nearly 45 percent of all reserve forces.[4]

▲ Major Tim Pfeifer is an Air Force reservist. When on duty with the 920th Rescue Wing, he flew an HH-60 Pave Hawk helicopter to search for survivors of Hurricane Katrina in New Orleans. When he is not on duty, Pfeifer is a pilot for American Airlines.

ANG and AFR airmen were fighting side-by-side
with their active duty counterparts more than ever
before and for longer periods of time. This meant
there was a larger strain on reservists' civilian
employers. Organizations such as the Employer
Support for Guard and Reserve (ESGR), first
organized in 1972, assist reservists and their civilian employers in dealing with the increased time
away from the office. The Uniformed Services
Employment and Reemployment Rights Act
(USERRA) provides job protection to National
Guard and Reserve members. It ensures that
employers do not discriminate against reservists.
USERRA also protects employers by ensuring they
are notified of deployments and gives them a five-
year limit to hold an employee's job.[5]

In addition to fighting terrorism in Iraq and
Afghanistan, the Air Force is fully involved in providing support to other missions overseas and to
homeland defense.

Operation Noble Eagle

The Air Force is the lead service for protecting
U.S. airspace through Operation Noble Eagle (ONE),
using ten Air National Guard fighter wings in three
air defense sectors around the nation. The Air Force
ensures that the United States is protected from any
possible aerial attack by flying combat air patrols
over major U.S. cities, and providing air support
for major events such as presidential inaugurations

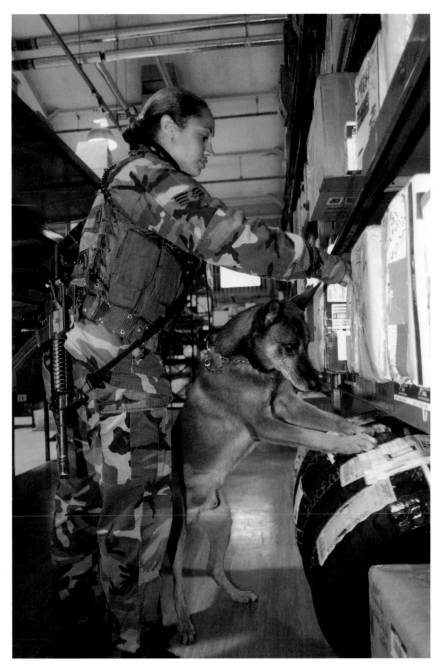

▲ Senior Airman Nicole Kaehler uses her trained dog, Harras, to search packages at the base post office for bombs after the September 11 terrorist attacks.

and the Superbowl. From September 11, 2001, through March 2003, Air National Guard, Air Force Reserve, and active Air Force participating in ONE flew more than 27,625 fighter, tanker, and airborne early-warning missions.[6]

Operation Joint Guardian

Since June 1999, the Air Force, as part of the U.S. European Command, has provided forces, aircraft, and logistical support to Operation Joint Guardian, the NATO-led peacekeeping operation in Kosovo. The NATO-led Kosovo Force (KFOR) includes forces from the United States, Great Britain, France, Germany, Italy, Czech Republic, Netherlands, Spain, Poland, Greece, Turkey, Russia, Canada, and Ukraine.[7]

Korea

Since the end of the Korean War in the 1950s, the United States has remained in South Korea. Known as the 7th Air Force, this fighting unit is based at Osan Air Base in South Korea. It includes F-16s based at Kunsan Air Base in South Korea, and A-10s, F-16s, HH-60G helicopters, and U-2 recon-naissance aircraft also stationed at Osan. Some airmen stationed at Osan Air Base have the choice of doing a one-year tour by themselves or a two-year tour where they can bring their family if they are married or have children. Those selecting a one-year tour are allowed to come home for one month after the first six months away.

Six

Structure of the Air Force

The Air Force is run by a civilian called the secretary of the Air Force. The military head of the Air Force is called the Air Force chief of staff and reports to the secretary of the Air Force. The Department of the Air Force consists of major commands, direct reporting units, and field operating units.

Each major command is made up of numbered air forces, which are made up of wings. A wing contains numerous groups, each of which is responsible for a function on a base, such as operations or medical. Groups are made up of squadrons and each squadron is made up of flights. Most wings have subunits located on a single Air Force base, although several have units located on multiple bases.

Major Commands

The Air Force has nine major commands, or MAJCOMs, two of which are overseas. Each

MAJCOM is responsible for a specific part of the Air Force, like training troops, fixing airplanes, or providing fighter and bomber forces.

Air Combat Command (ACC)

Air Combat Command is the largest MAJCOM and is headquartered at Langley Air Force Base in Virginia. ACC operates fighter, bomber, attack, reconnaissance, battle management, electronic-combat aircraft, and command-and-control systems. Some planes in ACC include the B-2 stealth fighter, the F-117 stealth fighter, and the F-22.

There are some one hundred thousand active duty airmen and more than ten thousand civilians assigned to ACC. In addition, more than fifty thousand Air National Guardsmen and more than ten thousand Air Force Reservists consider ACC their headquarters, bringing ACC's total to more than one hundred seventy thousand people.[1]

ACC has twenty-seven bases organized into four numbered air forces (1st Air Force, 8th Air Force, 9th Air Force, and 12th Air Force). ACC has three major subunits and a direct reporting unit called the Air and Space Expeditionary Force Center.

Air Education and Training Command (AETC)

AETC is headquartered at Randolph Air Force Base in Texas and conducts recruiting, training, and education for all Air Force airmen such as basic military training, technical training, flying training, and professional military and degree-granting professional education.

AETC also operates basic military training for enlisted members; the U.S. Air Force Academy, Reserve Officer Training Corps (ROTC), or Officer Training School (OTS) for officers; and flight training. Air University (AU) at Maxwell Air Force Base in Alabama is also part of AETC. AU is headquarters to the Air Force's programs for training officers like ROTC, Junior ROTC, and OTS; the Civil Air Patrol; officer and enlisted professional military education; and continuing education programs like the Air Force Institute of Technology, which is based at Wright Patterson Air Force Base in Ohio.

There are more than seventy-six thousand active duty, ANG, AFR, civilians, and contract workers in AETC.[2]

Air Force Materiel Command (AFMC)

Air Force Materiel Command, based at Wright Patterson Air Force Base, operates three major product centers that develop, acquire, test, and deploy air-delivered weapons, such as missiles and command-and-control systems used by commanders to fight wars. They also provide program management for everything from new weapons programs to retiring weapon systems.

AFMC operates air logistics and test centers like the Aircraft Maintenance and Regeneration Center,

Air Force Research Laboratory, Air Force Test Pilot School, and the Air Force School of Aerospace Medicine.

The command also runs the world-renowned Air Force Flight Test Center (AFFTC) at Edwards Air Force Base in California. The AFFTC provides aerospace research, development, test and evaluation, and support for the United States and its allies. It is commonly known as the home of the Air

Major Active-duty Air Force Bases (AFBs)

McChord AFB *AMC*
Fairchild AFB *AMC*
WA
Malmstrom AFB *AFSPC*
MT
OR
ID
Mountain Home AFB *ACC*
Minot AFB *ACC*
ND
Grand Forks AFB *AMC*
SD
Ellsworth AFB *ACC*
MN
WI
MI
NH
VT
ME
Hanscom AFB *AFMC*
MA
NY
RI
CT
Beale AFB *ACC*
Travis AFB *AMC*
CA
UT
Hill AFB *AFMC*
WY
F.E. Warren AFB *AFSPC*
NE
Offutt AFB *ACC*
IA
Andrews AFB *AMC*
Bolling AFB *DRU*
McGuire AFB *AMC*
NJ
Dover AFB *AMC*
DE
MD
Vandenberg AFB *AFSPC*
NV
Nellis AFB *ACC*
CO
Buckley AFB *AFSPC*
U.S. Air Force Academy *DRU*
Schriever AFB *AFSPC*
Peterson AFB *AFSPC*
KS
McConnell AFB *AMC*
MO
IL
Scott AFB *AMC*
Wright-Patterson AFB *AFMC*
IN
OH
WV
VA
KY
Langley AFB *ACC*
Seymour Johnson AFB *ACC*
Whiteman AFB *ACC*
TN
NC
Pope AFB *AMC*
Edwards AFB *AFMC*
Los Angeles AFB *AFMC*
NM
Luke AFB *AETC*
Kirtland AFB *AFMC*
Cannon AFB *ACC*
AZ
Holloman AFB *ACC*
Davis-Monthan AFB *ACC*
Vance AFB *AETC*
OK
Altus AFB *AETC*
Tinker AFB *AFMC*
AR
Little Rock AFB *AETC*
Columbus AFB *AETC*
Arnold AFB *AFMC*
SC
Shaw AFB *ACC*
Charleston AFB *AMC*
GA
Robins AFB *AFMC*
Moody AFB *ACC*
Sheppard AFB *AETC*
Goodfellow AFB *AETC*
TX
Laughlin AFB *AETC*
Randolph AFB *AETC*
Lackland AFB *AETC*
Brooks AFB *AFMC*
Dyess AFB *ACC*
Barksdale AFB *ACC*
LA
MS
Keesler AFB *AETC*
AL
Maxwell AFB *AETC*
Eglin AFB *AFMC*
Tyndall AFB *AETC*
Hurlburt AFB *AFSOC*
FL
Patrick AFB *AFSPC*
MacDill AFB *AMC*
Eielson AFB *PACAF*
AK
Elmendorf AFB *PACAF*
Hickam AFB *PACAF*
HI
N
W E
S

Force test pilot and was where Chuck Yeager broke the sound barrier in 1947.

Air Force Reserve Command (AFRC)

AFRC is the newest MAJCOM and is headquartered at Robins AFB in Georgia. Reservists, nicknamed "citizen airmen," perform nearly all the same functions as active duty airmen. There are more than one hundred twenty-five thousand airmen in AFRC in three numbered air forces (4th AF, 10th AF, and 22nd AF).[3] Westover Air Reserve Base, home to the 439th Airlift Wing and its massive C-5 Galaxy, is the Air Force's largest reserve base.

Most reservists are part-timers, meaning that they have regular civilian jobs and report to the base on one weekend per month for Unit Training Assembly and an additional fifteen annual tour days. Many are also Air Reserve Technicians (ARTs). ARTs are reservists who also work as military civilians during the week. Some have the same job during reserve weekends as they have during the workweek. The only difference is during the week they wear civilian clothes and do not follow normal military customs like saluting.

Air Force Space Command (AFSPC)

AFSPC has one of the fastest-growing missions in the Air Force: the use and control of space for military purposes. Based at Peterson AFB in Colorado, AFSPC has four primary missions: space-force enhancement, space application, space support, and space control. More specifically, AFSPC operates the ballistic missile portion of the nation's nuclear-deterrent forces, places communications satellites into space, conducts counterspace operations like surveillance, and operates early-warning facilities around the country to protect from space-based attack.

Air Force Special Operations Command (AFSOC)

With fewer than twenty thousand airmen, AFSOC is the smallest MAJCOM and provides America's specialized air power.[4] This includes missions like information warfare, rescue operations, and specialized refueling. AFSOC also conducts psychological operations in which information is used against the enemy to destroy its morale or will to fight. In Iraq, for example, AFSOC units dropped leaflets over enemy territory to inform soldiers and civilians they were fighting Saddam Hussein and not the Iraqi people. The leaflets also let them know how to surrender. AFSOC operates out of nine locations in the United States, Japan, and England.

Air Mobility Command (AMC)

The massive planes that carry troops and equipment or refuel other aircraft are part of the Air Mobility Command. AMC manages air mobility during wartime by providing airlift, air refueling, special

The Titan IV-B is the largest rocket used by the Air Force.

air missions, and medical-evacuation aircraft for U.S. forces.

At nearly one hundred fifty thousand strong, AMC aircraft fly more than forty-one thousand hours per month, bringing supplies or troops to the front lines in places like Iraq.[5] They also conduct air refueling to ensure aircraft can accomplish their missions without having to land to refuel. AMC operates the Air Force's aeromedical evacuation aircraft that bring wounded and dead U.S. service members back home. AMC is headquartered at Scott AFB in Illinois and has one numbered air force, 18th AF, also at Scott AFB.

Pacific Air Forces (PACAF)

PACAF operates out of Hickam Air Force Base in Hawaii and is the oldest of Air Force MAJCOMs. Established in 1944, PACAF organizes, trains, equips, and maintains resources to conduct air operations throughout the Asia-Pacific region during peacetime, crisis, and war. There are more than fifty-four thousand airmen in PACAF at places like Japan, South Korea, Alaska, and Guam.[6]

United States Air Forces in Europe (USAFE)

U.S. Air Forces in Europe is the Air Force's other overseas MAJCOM. USAFE, pronounced "you-say-fee," is headquartered at Ramstein Air Base in Germany. USAFE's area of responsibility spans 20.5 million square miles and ninety-three countries from the northern tip of Greenland, to the eastern tip of Russia, to the southern tip of Africa. There are more than forty-two thousand airmen assigned to USAFE at bases in England, Germany, Turkey, Italy, Iceland, and the Azores, a small chain of islands off the coast of Portugal.[7]

Direct Reporting Units

Direct reporting units (DRU) are subdivisions of the Air Force, and report to Air Force headquarters at the Pentagon. They are separate from any MAJCOM because they have unique missions, legal requirements, or other factors. There are five DRUs: the Air Force Academy; the 11th Wing at Bolling AFB near Washington, D.C., the Air Force's legal authority under the Uniform Code of Military Justice, which also provides ceremonial and musical support such as the Air Force Band and Air Force Honor Guard; the Doctrine Center at Maxwell AFB; the Operational Test and Evaluation Center at Kirkland AFB in New Mexico; and the Studies and Analyses Agency located at the Pentagon.

Field Operating Agencies

The Air Force operates thirty-two Field Operating Agencies (FOA), which are Air Force subdivisions carrying out activities under the control of a headquarters Air Force functional manager. One FOA is the Air Force Agency for Modeling and Simulation, based in Orlando, Florida. This agency develops new tactics and planning, and provides mission

▲ The Air Force Band's rock band "Systems Go" performs during a readiness exercise at Wright-Patterson Air Force base in Ohio.

rehearsal and training. Another FOA is the Air Force News Agency in San Antonio, Texas, which is the Air Force's main news service providing news and information to Air Force airmen around the world via print, radio, television, and the Internet.

Air National Guard and Reserve

When not called to active federal duty, Air National Guard (ANG) airmen are under the authority of the governors of the fifty states, Puerto Rico, Guam, the Virgin Islands, and the commanding general of the District of Columbia. Each governor is represented in the state or territory chain of command by an adjutant general. While ANG airmen train and prepare for war-related scenarios like the rest of the Air Force, governors can call them to preserve peace, order, and public safety. For example, they can provide assistance during emergencies, such as natural disasters and civil disturbances. ANG airmen conduct these missions because federal military troops are prohibited from conducting law enforcement activities in the United States. However, during wartime or threats to national security, the president has the authority to call up ANG airmen to active duty.

There are one hundred nine thousand ANG airmen playing a vital role in the overall Air Force mission. For example, the ANG provides 100 percent of the interceptor duties, 64 percent of the air-traffic control, 49 percent of the tactical airlift, 45 percent of the KC-135 refueling capability, 32 percent of the general-purpose fighter force, and 23 percent of the rescue-and-recovery capability.[8]

The Air Reserves provides airmen and aircraft usually during a national emergency. However, reservists also provide support in peacetime. It is divided into two sections: the Ready Reserve and the Standby Reserve. The Ready Reserve is called to fight in any emergency, while the Standby Reserve is called on in a time of war.

Seven

Women and Minorities in the Air Force

It is unlawful in the United States to discriminate against an individual or group because of their race, color, national origin, religion, or gender.[1] The Air Force promotes the equal treatment and role of women and minorities and recognizes their significant military contributions. Air Force Military Equal Opportunity (MEO) offices are on every Air Force Base to handle any issues related to discrimination or sexual harassment. All commanders and airmen must go through yearly MEO training.

Women in the Air Force

While women in the past did play support roles during military conflicts, they did not have an active role in flight operations. As a result, the first hurdle women had to cross was proving they were fit to fly. In the United States, Mary H. Myers set an altitude record in 1886 by soaring four miles above the earth in a balloon without oxygen equipment. American women, however, were initially barred from flying aircraft during World War I in England and the United States. In Europe, women were used as pilots almost from the beginning of the war. In Germany, women flew aircraft from factories to fields near the battlefronts. In Russia, women were given military ranks.[3] By the 1920s and 1930s, however, American women such as Amelia Earhart had captivated the country with their airborne feats.

Soon, Britain created a women's section of its Air Transport Auxiliary (ATA). Despite the fact that women faced discrimination, made less money than their male counterparts, and had to pay for their lodgings, the ATA flight records revealed that the accident rate for men and women was nearly identical.[4] During World War II, more than one hundred women were flying in the ATA.[5]

In 1941, pilot Jacqueline Cochran met Hap Arnold, a high-ranking Army Air Force officer, in Washington where he described the problem of ferrying bombers overseas. This job was being done by civilians since military pilots were needed for combat. Cochran suggested using women in this role. Arnold at first said he was not certain "whether a slip of a young girl could fight the controls of a B-17," but later agreed to allow Cochran to fly a bomber across the Atlantic on June 17, 1941.[6]

Arnold suggested Cochran fly with the ATA, and she brought a small group of women to Britain to train. To her surprise when she returned to America in 1942, she found out that Nancy Harkness Love was forming the Women's Auxiliary Ferrying Squadron (WAFS). Cochran organized a Women's Flying Training Detachment from a field in Houston to train pilots for eventual service in the WAFS. In May 1943, the group moved to Avenger Field in Sweetwater, Texas. The women lived in barracks under the same disciplinary rules as if they were actually in the military.[7]

On August 5, 1942, both groups merged, becoming the Women Airforce Service Pilots (WASP), led by Cochran. WASPs began to ferry aircraft to bases around the United States and became involved in many kinds of flying except combat.

Marty Volkomener trains to become a Women's Airforce Service Pilot in 1943.

The WASP program ended when male military pilots began returning to the United States and resumed the ferrying role. Because of the success of the WASPs, Arnold was in favor of keeping the women pilots. However, without authorization to make them part of the military, he could not. During its time, WASP graduated 1,074 of its 1,830 recruits. The women delivered 12,650 planes of 77 different types while suffering only 38 deaths.[8]

Things began to change in 1948 when Congress passed the Women's Armed Forces Integration Act.

Despite the fact the total air forces could not be made up of more than 2 percent by women and women could not be promoted above lieutenant colonel, women played a vital role in war. During the Korean War, Air Force nurses served as flight nurses in Korea. Many other servicewomen were assigned to duty in Japan and Okinawa.[9]

Public Law 90-130, which allowed the ANG to enlist women, was passed in 1968 and the first Air Force woman entered the ANG. A year later, the Air Force Reserve Officers Training Corps opened to women. In 1971, the first Air Force woman was promoted to brigadier general. In 1976, the Air

▲ Senior Airman Stephanie Ragan helps a fellow airman put on an oxygen mask during a test at Barksdale Air Force Base in Louisiana.

Eileen Marie Collins

Born on November 19, 1956, Colonel Eileen Collins became the first woman to command a Space Shuttle. Collins graduated in 1979 from Air Force Undergraduate Pilot Training and later became a C-141 pilot. She was selected for the astronaut program while attending the Air Force Test Pilot School. On July 23, 1999, she took the shuttle *Columbia* on a five-day mission to bring a powerful telescope to space to help study the universe.

She returned to space as commander of the shuttle *Discovery* on July 26, 2005. This was the first shuttle flight since the *Columbia* was destroyed while reentering Earth's atmosphere in February 2003. Her crew's mission was to test and evaluate new safety procedures put in place since the *Columbia* tragedy.[10]

Force Academy admitted the first female cadets and soon women began entering pilot training and Test Pilot School.

By the 1980s, women were involved in conflict, such as in Grenada during Operation Urgent Fury in 1983. In 1986, six Air Force women served as pilots, copilots, and boom operators on the KC-135 and KC-10 tankers that refueled FB-111s during the raid on Libya. That same year, the Air Force Academy's top graduate was a woman.

In 1989, 770 women participated in Operation Just Cause in Panama. Two earned the Air Medal with the "V" device that means they served in combat. During Operations Desert Shield and Desert Storm, over forty thousand Air Force women contributed to the missions. In 1991, Congress repealed the laws banning women from flying in combat.

In 1993, Dr. Sheila Widnall was the first woman to be named secretary of the Air Force and the first female service secretary in the history of the armed forces. During Operation Desert Fox in 1998, a woman was in the first wave of U.S. strikes against Iraq. By 2004, women in the Air Force were fighting the war on terrorism throughout the world in many roles. To date, women in the Air Force are still restricted from becoming pararescue troops or combat controllers and from serving in those units and positions that routinely operate with direct ground combat units.[11]

African Americans

African Americans also experienced challenges to being fully accepted into the military. That began to change in 1941 with the passing of Executive Order 8802, which prohibited discrimination within the military.

On July 19, 1941, the Army Air Force began a program in Tuskegee, Alabama, to train black Americans as military pilots at the Tuskegee Institute. The first classes of Tuskegee Airmen were trained to be fighter pilots.

Thirteen started in the first class and five completed the training. One of them was Captain Benjamin O. Davis, Jr., who became the Air Force's first black general. Another famous Tuskegee Airman was Daniel "Chappie" James, Jr., who would later become the Air Force's first black four-star general.

The Tuskegee Airmen began overseas combat

▲ Four Tuskegee airmen: from left, Benjamin O. Davis, Herbert E. Carter, Jr., Mac Ross, and Theopolis Moore. Davis became commander of the first all-African-American air unit. His father, Benjamin O. Davis, Sr., was the first African-American general in the U.S. Army.

operations near Naples, Italy, in February 1944, flying air patrols over Naples Harbor and the Mediterranean Sea. In April 1944, the group transferred to the Adriatic Sea side of Italy near Foggia, and began conducting long-range heavy bomber escort missions for the 15th Strategic Air Force. In July 1944, the 99th Fighter Squadron was transferred to Ramitelli and the group became the only four-squadron fighter group performing bomber escort missions in the 15th Air Force.

In September 1943, a training program began at Tuskegee to develop bomber pilots. However, World War II ended before these men were able to get into combat. By the end of the war, 992 men had graduated from pilot training at Tuskegee, 450 of whom were sent overseas for combat assignment. During the same period, approximately 150 lost their lives while in training or on combat flights.

The Tuskegee Airmen earned significant recognition primarily because their squadron never lost a bomber to enemy attacks. They flew 15,000 combat sorties and destroyed 111 German airplanes in the air and 150 on the ground.[12]

African Americans would continue to play a large role in future conflicts. Two African Americans would go on to earn the Medal of Honor during World War II, two during the Korean War, and twenty in the Vietnam War.

▲ Staff Sergeant Herbert Hayers, Jr., controls air traffic at Kunsan Air Force Base in Mississippi.

Today, African Americans make up approximately 15 percent of the Air Force population. Many have attained the rank of four-star general. One was General Lloyd "Fig" Newton who was the commander of AETC and the first African American to be selected for the U.S. Air Force Thunderbirds in 1974. This is a team of pilots that stages spectacular air demonstrations for the American public.

On May 15, 2005, African Americans in the Air Force reached another significant milestone when Colonel Stayce Harris became the first African-American woman to command a flying wing. She commanded the 459th Air Refueling Wing at Andrews Air Force Base in Maryland.

African Americans in the Air Force have also made their mark as astronauts. One was Lieutenant Colonel Michael P. Anderson who died on February 1, 2003, over the southern United States when space shuttle *Columbia* exploded and its crew perished during reentry. Anderson also flew aboard space shuttle *Endeavor* in January 1998.

Hispanics in the Air Force

Hispanics have also made significant contributions to national defense and have earned more Medals of Honor than any other ethnic minority. Hispanics have been part of the defense of America since the Revolutionary War.

In 1929, Lieutenant General Elwood Quesada, a Hispanic, proved the importance of air refueling. He was a member of the famous "Question Mark" crew along with Major Carl Spaatz and others, which set a sustained in-flight refueling record of 151 hours—more than six days in the air over Los Angeles. Air refuelings take place when a tanker aircraft provides fuel to another aircraft in-flight using hoses or "booms." The plane flew eleven thousand miles and was air-refueled forty-three times; nine times were at night.[13]

Some five hundred thousand Hispanics served in the U.S. armed forces during World War II. One, Oscar Perdomo, became the last ace of the conflict. Flying in a P-47N Thunderbolt near Okinawa on August 13, 1945, he encountered five Japanese aircraft and shot down three of them. Later, he spotted two Japanese trainer aircraft and shot one down before being "jumped" by three more. In the ensuing combat, Perdomo achieved his fifth confirmed kill of the day. This Hispanic-American hero joined the most elite in the fighter community, an ace in a day.[14]

During the Korean War, U.S. Air Force Captain

▲ Linda Garcia Cubero, the first Hispanic woman graduate of any service academy, finished the Air Force Academy and went on to a successful career in the Air Force and the corporate world.

Technical Sergeant Sator "Sandy" Sanchez

Technical Sergeant Sator "Sandy" Sanchez was a B-17 aerial gunner who volunteered to stay in combat even after reaching the required twenty-five combat missions. He flew a total of forty-four combat missions with the 95th Bomb Group. In recognition of his dedication, a B-17 was nicknamed *Smilin' Sandy Sanchez* in his honor. It is the only known B-17 aircraft ever named for an enlisted man. After a short rest in the United States, he volunteered for his third combat tour and was sent to the 15th Air Force in Italy. On March 15, 1945, he volunteered for his 66th and last mission. During the bombing run, his B-17 was hit and severely damaged. Everyone parachuted out of the plane except Sanchez. The B-17 exploded and crashed. Sanchez's body was never recovered.[16]

Manuel J. Fernandez, an F-86 fighter pilot, was credited with over 14 enemy kills in 125 missions. He was the third-ranked fighter pilot of the war and retired as a colonel.

In Vietnam, Air Force Master Sergeant Juan J. Valdez climbed aboard the last U.S. helicopter to depart the roof of the American Embassy in Saigon, ending the U.S. presence in Vietnam, which spanned eighteen years. Valdez's presence confirmed the Latino theme of participation in America's wars: "First in . . . last to leave."[15] Approximately eighty thousand Hispanics served in the Vietnam War.

Hispanics also served valiantly during the Persian Gulf War and today continue to serve in leadership positions fighting the war on terrorism.

One current pioneer is Lieutenant Colonel Edward Cabrera, who in 2005 was commander of the 411th Flight Test Squadron at Edwards Air

Force Base in California. Cabrera led an elite team of five of the best test pilots to gauge the war fighting abilities of the F/A 22 Raptor, the world's most advanced aircraft. As the United States' next generation air-dominance warplane, the Raptor has been given the role of maintaining and expanding the Air Force's superiority in the sky.

The Air Force's Policy on Homosexuals

Early in the 1992 presidential campaign, former President Bill Clinton promised that he would "lift the ban" on homosexuals serving in the military. The issue drew heated debate among policymakers and the public.

Some believed that homosexual conduct in the military represented an unacceptable risk to morale, good order and discipline, and unit cohesion—requirements that make military life different from civilian life. A policy was designed to balance both the unique demands of military life with the recognition that homosexuals have contributed to national defense. This policy was termed, "don't ask, don't tell," meaning service members would not be asked about their sexual orientation, as had previously been done on a form during enlistment in the Air Force. More specifically, the Department of Defense policy states that sexual orientation is a personal and private matter and should not prohibit someone from serving in the military service, but open homosexual conduct would not be allowed.

The policy also states that the armed services may not conduct an investigation to determine someone's sexual orientation. In 1980, prior to the policy, 1,754 people were forced to leave the military due to homosexual activity.[17] That number dropped to 770 in 2003.[18] The military policy toward homosexual conduct has been upheld by many courts, including the U.S. Supreme Court.

Other Minorities

In addition to women, Hispanics, and African Americans, the Air Force and the federal government also formally recognize other minority groups during special observances. They include Asian-Pacific heritage month in May, Disability Employment Awareness Month in October, and American Indian and Alaska Native Heritage Month in November. Air Force airmen come from nearly all countries around the world. For example, in January 2006, there were 290 active-duty enlisted airmen who were born in Colombia, 25 from Cambodia, 38 from Ethiopia, four from Iraq, and one from Papua New Guinea. They join an organization that recognizes and celebrates their cultural and ethnic differences.[19]

Eight

Life on an Air Force Base

Named for pioneers of flight, aviation heroes, or for a nearby town, Air Force bases are found throughout the United States and the world. Bases are often the town's largest employer, with both military personnel and civilians working on base, and often contribute hundreds of millions of dollars to the economy of surrounding communities.

Almost all Air Force bases resemble small U.S. towns. For starters, most bases have a shopping area with a department store and other smaller shops. Operated by the Army and Air Force Exchange Service (AAFES), the Base Exchange or BX, offers tax-free shopping.

In addition, AAFES operates barbershops, fast food restaurants and flower shops. Other vendors like vitamin shops, Internet cafés, and coffee shops also operate here. Most bases have restaurants; a grocery store, called the commissary; gas stations; and arts-and-crafts centers.

Charles Smith, the information and industrial security manager of the 22nd Security Forces Squadron, gets his hair cut at the BX on McConnell Air Force Base.

For entertainment, airmen can play golf on the base or watch a movie at the base movie theater. There are also bowling alleys and nightclubs on most bases. Since the Air Force promotes good physical conditioning, bases also offer gyms. Most have swimming pools and outdoor recreation facilities where airmen can rent boats and camping gear. Air Force bases also have facilities like schools, churches, and hospitals. Airmen living on base or near the base can have all the services they would normally find in a town.

Many airmen are also offered the opportunity to live on base. The only things airmen have to pay for are services like cable, telephone, and Internet access. Single enlisted members can stay in dorm-style rooms. Airmen with families are offered two- to four-bedroom houses on most bases.

Those who live off base are given a tax-free allowance to help pay for rent or a mortgage. The amount of the allowance is based on the airman's rank, the number of years in the Air Force, and location.

More Benefits

All Air Force airmen are given thirty days of vacation. When not in uniform, airmen can take advantage of travel opportunities offered on many military installations. For instance, airmen can hop a transport-type aircraft to many places around the world for free. Airmen and their families can fly to Hawaii from Travis Air Force Base in California, if there is space available on scheduled flights.

Those wishing to continue their education can sign up for college courses offered on base by different colleges and universities. The Air Force even offers a tuition-assistance program to help pay for school. The program pays 100 percent (up to $250 per semester hour or equivalent) of the cost of college courses to a maximum of $4,500 per year.[1]

The Montgomery G.I. Bill is also available to provide assistance in paying for school and provides

▲ First Lieutenant Rickie Banister of the 319th Missile Squadron competes during the 2005 Armed Forces Bowling Championships. Banister went on to win the competition.

▲ Chief Master Sergeant Donald Clabaugh (left) and Marine Corps Gunnery Sergeant Brian Hamilton are greeted by Secretary of the Air Force Dr. James G. Roche (right). Clabaugh and Hamilton were among the first enlisted students to get degrees from the Air Force Institute of Technology.

up to thirty-six months of benefits to those eligible. These benefits may be used for degree and certificate programs, flight training, apprenticeship or on-the-job training, and correspondence courses.

For enlisted members, the Air Force offers an associate's degree via the Community College of the Air Force. CCAF is America's largest community college and is the only degree-granting institution in the world dedicated entirely to Air Force airmen.

For officers wishing to get a master's or other advanced degree directly related to their specialty, the Air Force offers its own fully-paid graduate school for engineering and management degrees called the Air Force Institute of Technology.

Community Involvement

Since bases are often near major towns and cities—not to mention the fact the Air Force is funded through taxpayer dollars—the Air Force actively seeks ways to be involved in the community and open its doors to its neighbors. Each base has a public affairs office that is responsible for maintaining the public's trust and support for the base, the Air

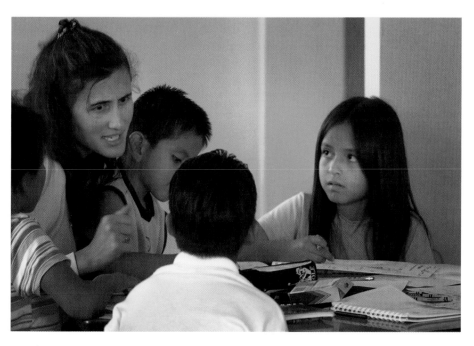

▲ Captain Sara Schwennesen, a public affairs officer, teaches English to Ecuadorian children who have come to America.

Force and the mission. One way Air Force public affairs offices do this is by inviting community groups on to the base for tours. In addition, most bases host airshows that often attract thousands of people to see aerial demonstrations and vintage aircraft and to converse with the Air Force men and women in uniform.

In addition to formal public affairs programs, Air Force airmen are actively involved in activities like Parent Teacher Associations, coaching, volunteering with churches and nonprofit organizations, as well as tutoring.

However, before anyone can do this as a United States airman, he or she must first take an important step. Joining the Air Force can be one of the biggest decisions in a young person's life.

Nine

Joining the Air Force

Whether a person wants to be an officer or enlisted airman, the surest way to prepare for service in the Air Force is to maintain good grades, good character, and good physical shape. Recruits have to be at least seventeen to apply and be in basic training before their twenty-eighth birthday. Air Force recruiters are found in nearly all cities and near most communities.

Enlisted

While it is possible to enlist with a general equivalency diploma (GED), generally one must be a high school graduate to join the Air Force. Recruits are given the Armed Services Vocational Aptitude Battery (ASVAB). The ASVAB is broken down into four categories: mechanical, administrative, general, and electronic. An overall score of 36 is the minimum qualifying score for a high school graduate and a 64 is required for someone with a GED.

Each career field has minimum score requirements. The ASVAB scores, along with results from a physical examination are reviewed during job counseling in the enlistment process.

Once accepted, Air Force recruits are sent to a Military Entrance Processing Station where they get a physical and eye exam, are weighed, and tested for drugs and diseases. Recruits are fingerprinted and interviewed by a counselor to help match the person's interest and ASVAB scores with the needs of the Air Force.

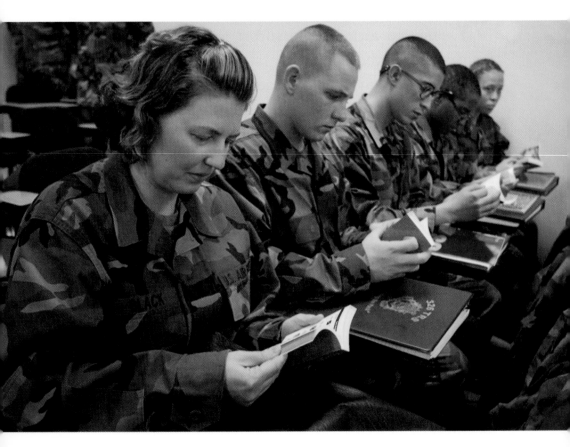

▲ New airmen read over their copies of the Airman handbook.

They are then sent to basic military training (BMT) at Lackland Air Force Base in Texas. The six-week course includes physical training, classroom instruction, field training, and instruction on Air Force customs.

From the minute trainees step off the bus, they are quickly prepared for the discipline they will need for the next six weeks and their entire Air Force career. They are assigned to a flight headed by a training instructor. When they first arrive, trainees are informally referred to as "rainbows" for the many colors they wear on their clothes and the color of their hair.

The first week is designed to provide many mental and physical challenges. Days begin at 5:00 A.M. and include classroom instruction, physical conditioning, and training on customs like how to salute.

Physical conditioning is a major part of BMT. Trainees must pass two physical conditioning tests that consist of running, push-ups, and sit-ups in order to graduate. Males must run two miles in less than 16 minutes and 45 seconds and do at least 50 sit-ups and 45 push-ups. Women must run the two miles in less than 19 minutes and 45 seconds and do at least 50 sit-ups and 27 push-ups.[1]

Throughout the next few weeks, trainees are taught about the Air Force structure, ethics, and values. They participate in field training and run an obstacle course that builds confidence. They are also given training on shooting and cleaning the M-16 rifle. Trainees can earn their first uniform ribbon by qualifying as an "expert" shooter.

In 1999, the Air Force introduced "Warrior Week" to prepare trainees for the reality of deployments they would likely face once on duty. Traditionally, the Air Force has not made a major effort to teach enlisted members soldiering skills. Since the Cold War ended, the Air Force has become smaller, but more airmen are being deployed to dangerous places. The Air Force estimates that 85 percent of all airmen entering service today will deploy to a world hot spot at least once during their career.

During Warrior Week, trainees learn how to build tents, put on chemical warfare protective equipment, and provide basic first aid. The whole exercise is built around an actual mission to defend the base from invasion by the enemy, a role played by the instructors.[2]

Following graduation, airmen are sent to technical

CAREER PROFILE

Master Sergeant Stephanie D. Clark

Master Sergeant Stephanie D. Clark was part of the 88th Aerial Port Squadron at McGuire AFB, New Jersey, when she was sent to support Operation Iraqi Freedom. She first went to Charleston AFB in South Carolina, where she led her section to an all-time record of moving more than 11,278 tons in 24 days aboard four types of aircraft bound for the war on terrorism. Three months later, she became the passenger service supervisor at Baghdad International Airport. Her work in moving 17,800 passengers got her selected as the non-commissioned officer in charge. She was responsible for all aspects of air logistics operations. After demobilization, coalition officials asked her to return to Iraq to instruct Iraqi police on techniques in counterterrorism and special operations.

▲ Two airmen look for opponents during Warrior Week.

training for the job, or specialty, they were assigned. Training is primarily conducted at Keesler AFB in Mississippi, or in Texas at Goodfellow AFB, Lackland AFB, or Sheppard AFB. For example, those entering computer-related fields normally go to Keesler AFB for training. Some specialized training can occur on the bases of other armed services, such as the Defense Information School at Fort Meade in Maryland for those entering the public affairs career field. Depending on the specialty, training can take a few weeks to a full year. Following this technical training, airmen are sent to their first duty station.

Enlisted Benefits

Enlisted airmen earn a salary based on rank and number of years in the Air Force. They are paid twice per month. Enlisted ranks go from airman basic (E-1) through chief master sergeant (E-9). For example, in 2006 an airman basic with four months in the Air Force earned a base salary of about $1,200 per month. A chief master sergeant with twenty-six years in the Air Force earned about $5,400 per month.

However, basic pay is only one part of the pay equation. The Air Force pays bonuses for many career fields where there are shortages of people or the jobs are very stressful. Single enlisted airmen are also provided free room and board and a clothing allowance; some earn hazardous-duty or foreign-language pay. Married airmen living off base are provided money for food and housing. These allowances are tax free. Airmen also have a generous retirement plan where they can retire with up to 50 percent of their final base salary after twenty years of active duty service. The Air Force also provides $500,000 in life insurance benefits for less than $20 per month.

After factoring in the free medical and dental benefits, a gym, tax-free shopping, educational benefits, and recreation programs, some consider the total compensation package in the Air Force very attractive and competitive with other career choices.

Airmen also have an opportunity to be promoted to higher ranks. Each year, airmen are evaluated by

Ranks and Salaries of Enlisted Airmen

Pay Grade	Rank	Approximate Salary*	Insignia
E-1	Airman Basic	under 4 months: $1,175 per month over 4 months: $1,270 per month	No insignia
E-2	Airman	$17,100 per year	
E-3	Airman First Class	$18,000–20,400 per year**	
E-4	Senior Airman	$19,200–24,000 per year	
E-5	Staff Sergeant	$21,600–30,000 per year	
E-6	Technical Sergeant	$24,000–36,000 per year	
E-7	Master Sergeant***	$27,600–49,200 per year	
E-8	Senior Master Sergeant***	$39,600–55,200 per year	
E-9	Chief Master Sergeant***	$48,000–64,800 per year	

* Approximate salaries are as of 2006 and do not include food and housing allowances, free healthcare, money for college, and bonuses.
** Salary for ranks E-3 through E-9 depend on the number of years in service.
*** A diamond in the insignia denotes First Sergeant status as well.

Air Force Medals

Name	Description	Medal
Afghanistan Campaign Medal	For serving in Afghanistan on or after October 24, 2001	
Air Force Cross	For extraordinary heroism, not justifying the Medal of Honor	
Airmen's Medal	For heroism, usually where one risks his or her life, not involving actual combat	
Bronze Star	For heroic service not involving aerial flight	
Defense Distinguished Service Medal	Awarded to high-ranking military officers	
Distinguished Flying Cross	For heroism while participating in aerial flight	
Distinguished Service Medal	For exceptional service	
Global War on Terrorism Service Medal	For serving in the Global War on Terrorism	
Iraq Campaign Medal	For serving in Operation Iraqi Freedom	
Medal of Honor	The highest honor someone serving in the military can receive	
Purple Heart	For being injured or killed in the line of duty	
Silver Star	For brave action against the enemy	

their supervisors in an Enlisted Performance Review. Promotions are also based, in part, on awards and decorations. Medals include the Defense Service Medal and the Medal of Honor, and the more common Good Conduct Medal, Achievement Medal, and Meritorious Service Medal. Many who have performed with honor while in direct contact with the enemy have earned the Bronze Star. Those hurt or killed in action are awarded the Purple Heart.

Officer

A commissioned officer in the Air Force must have at least a four-year college degree. Officers fill unit command and operational career fields such as pilots; navigators; and battle management managerial, professional, and technical jobs. Officers take the Air Force Officer Qualifying Test (AFOQT), a test similar to the SAT. The AFOQT is used to select applicants for officer commissioning programs, such as the Air Force Academy, Officer Training School (OTS) or Air Force Reserve Officer Training Corps (ROTC). It is also used for selection into specific training programs such as pilot and navigator training.

The AFOQT can generally only be taken twice and candidates must wait 180 days between tests. Certain career fields have minimum scores. For example, to be a pilot you must score a 25 on the pilot section, which measures knowledge of aviation and mechanical systems, the ability to read aircraft instruments, and other flight-related knowledge.

Air Force Academy

Located in Colorado Springs, Colorado, the USAFA is one of the nation's premier undergraduate institutions. Cadets complete four years of studies and earn a bachelor of science degree. Emphasis is placed on academics, military training, athletic conditioning, and spiritual and ethical development.

Academics include classes in science, engineering, social sciences, and military studies. Cadets can specialize in any of thirty majors. USAFA has seventeen men's and ten women's intercollegiate sports teams that compete nationally. The physical education program consists of mandatory courses and electives ranging from judo to SCUBA.

The Honor Code is the centerpiece of a cadet's moral and ethical development. Cadets pledge: "We will not lie, steal, or cheat, nor tolerate among us anyone who does." All cadets take formal courses and instruction on honor and ethics.[3]

Following graduation, cadets are commissioned as second lieutenants. Most must make a five-year commitment to the active duty Air Force. Pilots must make a ten-year commitment.

The USAFA is selective, and the process of getting accepted starts early with good grades, extracurricular activities, and good leadership traits. About 85 percent of USAFA cadets finished in the top quarter of their high school class, and 11 percent graduated first in their class.

The average cadet scored a 1290 on the two-part

SAT. On the ACT, the cadet mean for English is 28 and 30 for both reading and mathematics. Candidates should meet with their guidance counselor to schedule the Preliminary Scholastic Aptitude Test (PSAT) as a sophomore in high school and should take the SAT or ACT during their junior year.[4]

▲ Air Force Academy graduates throw their caps in the air in celebration.

Candidates must also meet with an Air Force Academy Admissions Liaison Officer (ALO) or an Academy representative. During an interview with one of them, you may ask any questions you have about the Academy and speak directly with the people who will review your record. Guidance counselors have the names of local ALOs.

Finally, to increase the chances of being selected, candidates should obtain a nomination from their U.S. representative, one of their U.S. senators, or the vice president. Each member of Congress and the vice president may have five nominated cadets at the Air Force Academy at any one time. They may nominate up to ten candidates for each vacancy. Vacancies occur when cadets graduate or leave prior to graduation. The academy also reserves a select number of spots for international applicants and applicants from U.S. territories and military-affiliated categories.

ROTC

Air Force Reserve Officer Training Corps (ROTC) is open to full-time students at the 144 colleges and universities with detachments. There are also more than one thousand cross-town schools, which are affiliated with detachments at area universities. Those choosing to enroll at one of the crosstown schools would attend ROTC classes at the host university.

ROTC is the largest supplier of officers to the armed forces.[5] Credit for a portion of the first year

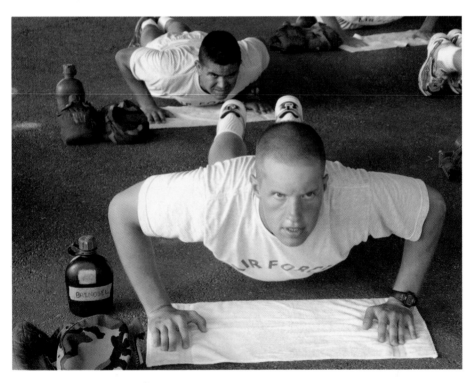

▲ ROTC cadets do push-ups during afternoon physical training.

of the four-year program may be provided for completion of at least two years of junior ROTC, a high school version of the program, participation in the Civil Air Patrol, military school training, or prior U.S. military service.

More than sixty-five hundred scholarships are available and pay for either full or partial tuition, books, laboratory fees, and extra spending money that increases each year in the program. While scholarships are available for any degree program, those with scientific- and technical-related majors have priority.[6] The deadline to apply for a scholarship is December 15 for high school seniors.

Those already in college can also join ROTC if they have at least a 2.5 GPA and are a U.S. citizen by the time they would graduate. They must also pass the AFOQT and a physical fitness test and meet the ROTC weight and body fat standards. They must also pass a physical examination and review board.

Finally, cadets cannot be conscientious objectors, who would not participate in war or take up arms because of religious training or beliefs.

Once accepted, cadets who are underclassmen (freshmen and sophomores) enter the General Military Course (GMC), which covers the development of airpower and Air Force structure. Students take courses in Aerospace Studies. AS100 is the student's first introduction to the Air Force. The AS200 course focuses on the history of airpower and how politics can affect the use of military power.

Upperclassmen enter the Professional Officer Course (POC), which covers Air Force leadership and management, as well as U.S. defense policy. AS300 discusses the skills needed to be a successful leader and manager. Case studies on leadership are discussed and cadets are given problem-solving exercises. AS400 examines national security, methods of managing conflict, alliances and regional security agreements, and analysis of the threats of war.

In addition to academic classes, both GMC and POC cadets participate in Leadership Laboratory.

▲ A cadet at the Air Force Academy crawls through muddy water, trying to keep her weapon dry, while on the assault training course.

Called "Lead Lab" for short, it provides cadets with an opportunity to develop leadership skills and apply what they learned in the classroom. Cadets are introduced to Air Force customs, courtesies, drills, and ceremonies like marching and how to properly wear the uniform. Cadets often take field trips to Air Force bases or have Air Force officers speak to them about their careers and experiences.[7]

During the summer between the sophomore and junior year, cadets are sent to field training, the ROTC version of BMT. This is a four- or six-week course that exposes cadets to military life and teaches them about leadership. This intensive course challenges cadets mentally and physically. After successful completion of field training, cadets return to campus and sign an Air Force contract to continue in the program. Cadets can take ROTC for two years and go through field training before they have to formally sign a contract and make a commitment to the Air Force.

After graduation, cadets are commissioned as second lieutenants in the Air Force and usually enter one of the career choices they have indicated they would like to fill. Those selected as pilots must serve ten years after completing a 49-week flight training course. Navigators must serve five years after navigator training plus a two-year inactive reserve commitment. Nonflying officers serve four years of active duty with a four-year inactive reserve commitment.

OTS

The third primary way to be commissioned an officer in the U.S. Air Force is through the Officer Training School at Maxwell AFB in Alabama. OTS has the mission of "Building today's leaders for tomorrow's Air Force."

OTS provides a twelve-week basic officer training (BOT) course programmed to train and commission one thousand officers annually. Additionally, OTS conducts a four-week commissioned officer training (COT) program to teach leadership skills to more than fifteen hundred new judge advocates, chaplains, and medical officers each year. Officer Training School is for those with the talent and drive to become a leader in the Air Force.[8]

Officer Pay and Benefits

Because of their added responsibility and account-ability, officers are compensated more than enlisted members. This is not to say enlisted members are less important.

Officer rank goes from second lieutenant to general. Each rank has an associated pay grade. For example, a second lieutenant is an O-1, a first lieu-tenant an O-2, and so on all the way to general, an O-10. There are four different types of generals. A brigadier general has one star, a major general two stars, a lieutenant general three stars, and a general has four stars on his or her uniform.

Officers in careers such as pilots, navigators,

Ranks and Salaries of Officers

Pay Grade	Rank	Approximate Salary per year*	Insignia
O-1	Second Lieutenant	$28,800–36,000	
O-2	First Lieutenant	$32,400–45,600	
O-3	Captain	$38,400–62,400	
O-4	Major	$43,200–73,200	
O-5	Lieutenant Colonel	$50,400–86,400	
O-6	Colonel	$61,200–105,600	
O-7	Brigadier General	$82,800–120,000	
O-8	Major General	$99,600–135,600	
O-9	Lieutenant General	$140,400–$150,000	
O-10	General	$160,800–$170,400	

* Salaries are as of 2006 and do not include food and housing allowances, free healthcare, money for college, and bonuses; also, an approximate salary range has been given for each rank.

and doctors receive extra special duty pay to help ensure their pay is similar to their civilian counterparts. Otherwise, it would be difficult to recruit officers in these careers that pay high salaries in the civilian world.

Similar to enlisted members, officers have a retirement plan; are provided hazardous-duty pay if warranted; get life insurance, medical and dental coverage; and receive other benefits, such as travel and thirty days of vacation time.

Risks

While the benefits and pay are appealing, the Air Force is not without its challenges and risks. Many recruits do not make it through basic training for reasons both physical and mental. In addition, the Air Force is focused on mobility, meaning the ability to move its forces and people to areas around the world. As a result, most airmen will at one point or another find themselves in direct support of an overseas conflict. In the past, pilots were most at risk of being killed by the enemy in combat. Today, the Air Force is playing a more operational role. This means people who are not pilots are also being sent to the front lines. So, anyone who joins the Air Force could be deployed to an area where airmen are in danger of being killed or injured.

Once one has weighed the risks and rewards and has decided to join the Air Force, there are a number of career opportunities that await.

Ten

Careers in the Air Force

It is likely that there is an Air Force career field that matches anyone's interests. Enlisted members can choose from one of 150 different career choices. Officers have forty-seven primary career choices. Pilots only make up about 4 percent of the Air Force, so there are many more opportunities in the Air Force than just flying.

Enlisted Opportunities

Enlisted opportunities fall into one of four main career areas: mechanical, administrative, general, and electronics.

Mechanical Careers

The Air Force develops and operates some of the most sophisticated and complicated equipment and is in need of those with the mechanical skills to run them. Airmen in a mechanical career field could be working as an aircraft mechanic or with radio systems, munitions, or vehicles.

Aircraft mechanics, for example, do everything from repairing engines to inspecting and operating ejection seats. Aircraft mechanics are the backbone of the flying operation and are a major reason the planes get off the ground. Mechanics work in crews and are usually assigned to a particular type of airplane, which they get to know better than their own automobiles.

There are also unique opportunities in this career area such as being an aerial gunner on an airplane or helicopter. Aerial gunners perform missions like operating a weapon system on a helicopter while looking for a downed pilot. They are placed on flying status as an aircrew member, which means they earn more through flight and hazardous duty pay.

Another unique job is a missile and space systems maintenance apprentice, who maintains, assembles, and inspects the Intercontinental Ballistic Missiles (ICBMs). ICBMs are always on alert to

CAREER PROFILE

Staff Sergeant Aaron D. Davenport

Staff Sergeant Aaron D. Davenport, an Explosive Ordnance Disposal equipment technician, deployed to Iraq six months after returning from duty in Afghanistan. He earned an Air Force Achievement Medal for his actions during covert recovery of a downed C-130 aircraft. He destroyed twelve 120mm mortar tubes in hidden weapons caches. His role in eliminating from a playground seventy-seven bomblets, which are small bombs dropped from a larger bomb, ensured the safety of five hundred Iraqi children. Working with the U.S. Army, he helped dispose of more than eighty-three thousand Iraqi munitions. He was a key player in support of a Marine Corps raid on an Iraqi surface-to-air missile battery, resulting in the destruction of seven SA-7 missiles. He also helped remove weapons caches endangering two thousand coalition forces in Saudi Arabia.

respond against enemies thousands of miles away. However, they are only effective if they are well maintained.

Administrative Careers

Administrative careers cover the many day-to-day base operations such as food, equipment, and housing that are critical to Air Force operations.

One career is airfield management, which plays a major role in a pilot's ability to land, take off, and taxi on runways and taxiways throughout the world. Airfield managers inspect airfields worldwide, monitor airfield construction projects, and issue notices to airmen for flight hazards or restrictions at the airfield or in the airspace that would pose flight-safety problems. If the airfield managers say something is not safe, all flying stops.

General Careers

The Air Force offers seventy-two types of general careers that are less mechanical in nature. These can include working in air traffic control, speaking foreign languages as a linguist, or collecting and analyzing intelligence.

General careers can also be in the medical field where airmen could work at a laboratory, in a clinic or pharmacy, or as medical-support persons inside an emergency room or in a war zone helping to treat wounded airmen. For example, an aeromedical apprentice assists in the care of patients during emergency medical flights as an airborne emergency medical technician (EMT). An aeromedical apprentice works closely with the flight surgeon to ensure that pilots and navigators, missile alert crewmembers, and air traffic control airmen are ready for duty. They also assist in minor surgical procedures.

While an aerial gunner would help protect the aircraft and a downed pilot during a combat search and rescue mission, it is the job of the pararescue apprentice to physically rescue a downed aircrew member. Pararescuemen also provide specialized aerospace rescue and recovery support for NASA's space shuttle flights. They are certified scuba divers and skilled in surface water operations—both scuba and amphibious, and are trained as combat medics. This is one of the few career fields open only to men.

Electronics Careers

As electronics become smaller and more powerful, they are increasingly used in Air Force weapon systems. Airmen in an electronics career field are trained to work with radar, avionics systems, surveillance systems, and missile and space systems.

▲ Staff Sergeant Carmen Jones uses a radarscope to coordinate aircraft movement. She is part of the 374th Operations Support Squadron.

After training at either Lackland AFB or Sheppard AFB in Texas, a bomber avionics systems instrument and flight control apprentice would perform operational checks and fix malfunctions of flight control systems on either the B-2 stealth bomber or the B-1. He or she is responsible for several of the advanced bomber's aircraft systems, including the automatic pilot, flight controls, navigation, and hydraulic system indicators.

Weather plays a significant role in successful military operations. Without accurate weather predictions, missions could be jeopardized because planes might not take off or land safely or targets might not be visible to nonradar or satellite-guided munitions. A weather apprentice analyzes and forecasts weather and space conditions for military decision-makers. Air Force weather apprentices receive training to understand the Earth's atmosphere and how to predict changes using satellite, radar, and computers.

Officer Opportunities

Officers also have a wide variety of specialties from which to choose. They typically fall into four career paths: flight, non-technical, specialty, and technical.

Flight Careers

Without flying there would be no Air Force. Air crews, however, are not just pilots. There are opportunities as a navigator, air battle-manager, radar navigator, and weapons navigator.

Pilots or navigators could be flying in a fighter, reconnaissance, surveillance, bomber, or airlift aircraft. However, aviation careers do not stop at the edge of the atmosphere. Officers can also compete to enter the astronaut program.

Those selected as pilot candidates attend the fifty-two week Joint Specialized Undergraduate Pilot Training (JSUPT). Civilian flight instructors conduct this training in aircraft such as the Cessna 152. Students receive fifty hours of instruction and must qualify for a private pilot certificate.

The JSUPT program is conducted with the Navy at Vance AFB in Oklahoma and Naval Air Station Whiting Field in Florida. Students complete primary flight training in the Air Force's T-37B and the Navy's T-34. Other students complete the primary

▲ An F-15 patrols the sky over Washington, DC.

training at Columbus AFB in Mississippi, or Laughlin AFB in Texas, flying the T-37B.

After the first part of JSUPT, students move on to advanced training. Students selected for fighter-bomber planes train in the T-38A. Those selected as airlift-tanker pilots complete their training in the T-1A at Columbus AFB in Mississippi, Laughlin AFB in Texas, or Vance AFB in Oklahoma, where they learn about air-to-air refueling, airdrop missions, and navigation.

Students selected to fly the C-130 Hercules train in the T-44 turboprop trainer at Naval Air Station Corpus Christi in Texas. Other students are selected to fly helicopters and complete their training at Fort Rucker in Alabama, in the UH-1 Huey. Helicopter training includes skills such as low-level flying.[1]

Non-technical Careers

These non-technical positions require people who can take charge and demonstrate leadership. Opportunities are available in areas such as intelligence, personnel, security forces, and communications. There are also opportunities as a space operations officer controlling one of the Air Force's multibillion-dollar space systems or helping to launch a wide range of satellites into orbit.

One unit, the 7th Space Warning Squadron at Beale AFB in California, works inside a ten-story, pyramid-like structure that itself is a radar system called Precision Acquisition of Vehicle Entry Phased

Array Warning System (PAVE PAWS). It is a fancy way of saying that they continuously scan the horizon to detect and track sea-launched ballistic missiles (SLBMs) and intercontinental ballistic missiles (ICBMs) headed toward North America.

Fortunately, there have been no enemy missiles for them to track, so the men and women of PAVE PAWS have another mission: to provide space surveillance and track objects in Earth's orbit. Their data is used to create a satellite catalog database that includes more than twenty-seven thousand man-made objects in orbit. About nine thousand of them require careful watching so they do not collide with satellites or space shuttles.[2]

Specialty Careers

These careers are highly specialized jobs that require specific skills such as judge advocates, special investigative officers, and band officers.

This career path also includes base chaplains who provide religious support to Air Force airmen. Chaplains develop and administer chaplain service policies; provide professional religious support; and advise commanders on religious, ethical, moral, morale, and quality-of-life issues. Chaplains also offer ministry to the many religious beliefs found in a military community. Active duty and Reserve chaplains are responsible for supporting the free exercise of religion for all airmen, their dependents, and other people authorized on base.

Technical Careers

While not many specialties fall under this category, technical careers are critical to the mission success of the Air Force. These careers include acquisition manager, aerospace engineer, mechanical engineer, scientist, and weather officer.

One specialty that has become increasingly important in the Air Force is the civil engineer. Often, the Air Force enters an area overseas without any infrastructure, which the Air Force refers to as a "bare base" location. Civil engineers build and maintain the buildings and utilities to operate a new location and specialize in areas including architectural, electrical, mechanical, and environmental engineering. They turn the bare base into a hustling and bustling installation complete with sleeping quarters; command-and-control buildings; functioning runways; and working water, power, and other utilities. Civil engineers also dispose of conventional, nuclear, and chemical weapons.

Many civil engineers, both officer and enlisted, attend the Air Force Combat Ammunition Center (AFCOMAC) training program, commonly referred to as "Ammo University." Located at Beale AFB in California, this course was developed to provide advanced training in combat ammunition planning and production.[3]

Future of the Air Force

The future of the Air Force remains bright and strong thanks in part to more advanced weapon systems, better integrated communication and control, and better trained airmen. The Air Force also continues to reduce its numbers and close bases.

Today, there are no military forces around the world that can take on the Air Force in direct combat. This means that future wars will continue to be smaller in scale than the two world wars. Enemies around the globe will continue to fight the United States using terrorism or attacking with unconventional weapons, such as computer viruses or chemical and biological weapons. As a result, the Air Force must be a responsive force and remains committed to the Air Expeditionary Force (AEF) concept. There are about thirty thousand airmen deployed all around the world as part of an AEF.[1]

In addition, the Air Force continues to include

▲ The Personnel Halting and Stimulation Response (PHaSR) gun is a non-lethal weapon developed by the Air Force that temporarily blinds an enemy.

space operations in military planning. The Air Force has taken the lead in making space the new battlefront. Space systems were an integral part of Operation Enduring Freedom and Operation Iraqi Freedom. For example, airmen used satellite feeds to identify and strike the broadcast capabilities of Iraqi state-run television. This space-based information was sent to Predator unmanned aerial vehicles that then fired Hellfire missiles in an effort to destroy the key source of Saddam Hussein's propaganda.[2]

One newer unit is the 527th Space Aggressor

Squadron based at Schriever Air Force Base in Colorado. The unit was activated in October 2000 to realistically play "the bad guys" during training exercises that teach space operators ways to defend space capabilities such as communications, surveillance, and navigation systems from enemy attack.[3]

Protecting information and communications systems will also be an area of increasing importance for the Air Force. Because the Air Force relies on computers and networks for nearly all of its functions, they are an area of possible enemy attack. Viruses, deception, and illusions are some ways enemies could conduct information warfare.

The Air Force continues to develop newer aircraft, weapon systems, and technologies to give airmen the edge in combat. Some, like unmanned aerial vehicles (UAV), help airmen avoid flying into highly defended enemy airspace altogether. A UAV is a drone that is piloted by remote control or through programs in its computer system.

One UAV, called Predator, is used to conduct reconnaissance over hostile territory. It is equipped with cameras that can transmit live footage of enemy actions to a commander on the ground or a fighter aircraft overhead. This information allows commanders to take out targets faster than ever before.

Because of their success in places like Kosovo, the Air Force began adding lasers on UAVs to "paint," or identify, a target. A laser-guided bomb delivered from an aircraft like the F-117 stealth

▼ This MQ-1 Predator is armed with an AGM-114 Hellfire missile.

fighter could then follow the laser beam and take out the target with incredible accuracy.

In the late 1990s, the Air Force began testing UAVs armed with Hellfire missiles in combat in Iraq. The results were mixed. The Predator performed well but the Hellfire missile was not a big enough weapon to take out large targets. However, this test encouraged the Air Force to continue to develop armed UAVs.

Another UAV called RQ-4 Global Hawk made its debut during the war in Afghanistan in 2002. It flies at altitudes above sixty thousand feet and will likely replace the U-2 Dragonlady. It does not shoot live video like the Predator but can capture images at night or through bad weather. It can fly for nearly a day and a half without refueling and can beam its images in real-time to battlefield commanders or other platforms.[4] The Air Force is also developing a bomber version of a UAV called a UCAV (unmanned combat air vehicle).

In addition, the F-22 will soon be streaking across the sky in combat. After years of testing, the

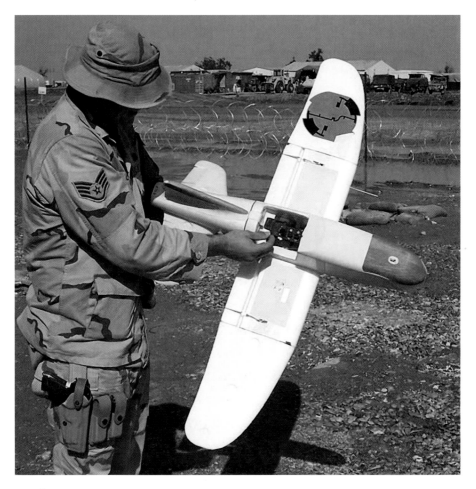

▲ The Desert Hawk is a miniature unmanned aerial vehicle that uses a camera to spot an approaching enemy.

F-22 was declared ready for war in December 2005, and will be based initially at Langley AFB in Virginia, home to the famed 1st Fighter Wing. The F-22 will replace the F-15 as the premier air-to-air fighter.

Another emerging weapon system is the YAL-1A airborne laser aircraft, which is a 747 aircraft that carries a laser designed to shoot down ballistic missiles in their take-off phase, when they are still over enemy territory. The megawatt-class chemical oxygen iodine laser (COIL) produces a beam powerful enough to burn a small hole in the missile. Because a missile uses extreme pressure during take-off, a slight hole in the missile would result in an explosion.

These technological advancements are designed to be used with other services since the Air Force is only one branch of the U.S. military. Training exercises such as the Combined Joint Training Force Exercise (CJTFEX), run out of Langley AFB, put the other U.S. military elements together with forces from the United Kingdom, Canada, the Netherlands, Norway, France, Germany, and Peru to train using realistic scenarios.

However, the Air Force recognizes that no weapon, system, or aircraft is sophisticated enough to operate without people. As a result, taking care of airmen continues to be the Air Force's top priority. Airmen carry out the mission and ensure the success and future of the U.S. Air Force.

The Air Force is looking at the factors that affect

▲ An F-22A Raptor fighter plane flies over Tucson, Arizona.

recruiting and retention to ensure the right people enter the Air Force and the right people remain. Many career fields are highly stressed, meaning they have few people filling positions that are in high demand. The Air Force will add more people to these career fields through recruiting and retraining airmen from other career fields.

Former Air Force chief of staff General John Jumper said in a letter to the troops:

> Saddam Hussein buried his airplanes in the sand rather than face your Air Force. . . . That's respect, and you continue to earn it every day. We will continue to remain closely engaged on these issues to ensure that we reshape the force into one that is suited for the 21st century while sustaining the standards of excellence and morale that are emblematic of the world's greatest Air Force.[5]

Wright brothers fly again in 1907

1941–1945

1943

December 17, 1903—The Wright Brothers make first powered airplane flight.

June 20, 1941—Creation of the Army Air Force (AAF) headed by Major General H.H. Arnold.

July 19, 1941—AAF begins program in Tuskegee, Alabama, to train African Americans as military pilots.

December 1, 1941—Creation of the Civil Air Patrol (CAP).

December 7, 1941—Japanese attack on Pearl Harbor in Hawaii.

December 8, 1941—U.S. declares war on Japan.

April 18, 1942—America strikes back at Japan during "Doolittle Raid."

August 17, 1942—The 97th Bomb Group makes first U.S. heavy bomber raid in Europe when twelve B-17s attack a railroad yard in France.

August 4, 1943—Women Airforce Service Pilots (WASP) formed with Jacqueline Cochran as director.

June 6, 1944—With support from the AAF, U.S. troops storm Normandy, France, on "D-day."

May 8, 1945—The Nazis are defeated and the war in Europe ends, on "V-E day."

August 6, 1945—A B-29, the *Enola Gay*, drops an atomic bomb over Hiroshima.

August 9, 1945—Another B-29, *Bockscar*, drops a second atomic bomb over Nagasaki.

August 15, 1945—Japan surrenders.

September 18, 1947—The Air Force becomes its own service.

1945

Oct. 14, 1947—Chuck Yeager becomes first man to fly faster than the speed of sound.

June 26, 1948—Operation Vittles, the first mission of the Berlin Airlift, begins.

July 1, 1949—Segregation in the Air Force ends.

June 25, 1950—Thousands of North Koreans storm South Korea starting the Korean War.

1950s

May 29, 1952—First Air Force combat use of air-to-air refueling.

July 27, 1953—Korean War ends.

October 14, 1962—Two Air Force U-2s take photographs of Soviet missile construction in Cuba.

February 8, 1965—The Air Force conducts its first retaliatory air strike in North Vietnam.

March 2, 1965—The Air Force begins Operation Rolling Thunder bombing campaign against North Vietnam.

1965–1975

1975

March 17, 1971—Jane Leslie Holley becomes the first woman commissioned through the Air Force Reserve Officer Training Corps program.

May 10, 1972—Operation Linebacker begins during the Vietnam War.

April 29, 1975—American involvement in South Vietnam ends.

September 1, 1975—General Daniel "Chappie" James becomes first African-American four-star general.

May 28, 1980—Ninety-seven women graduate from the U.S. Air Force Academy.

April 14, 1986—Air Force launches Operation Eldorado Canyon against Libyan leader Muammar Qadhafi.

1988

November 10, 1988—The Air Force reveals the existence of the F-117 stealth fighter.

June 10, 1989—Captain Jacqueline S. Parker becomes the first female pilot to graduate from U.S. Air Force Test Pilot School.

December 20, 1989—Operation Just Cause begins to oust Manuel Noriega. It is the largest night-combat airdrop since the Normandy invasion in 1944.

August 2, 1990—Saddam Hussein's forces invade Kuwait.

August 7, 1990—Operation Desert Shield begins.

1991

January 17, 1991—Operation Desert Storm begins with an all-out air assault.

February 28, 1991—Operation Desert Storm ends.

April 12, 1993—Operation Deny Flight, the air campaign against Bosnia-Herzegovina, begins.

August 6, 1993—Dr. Sheila E. Widnall becomes the first female armed services secretary.

1993

February 10, 1994—Lieutenant Jeannie Flynn, the first female Air Force combat pilot, completes F-15 training.

February 3, 1995—Air Force Lieutenant Col. Eileen M. Collins becomes the first female space shuttle pilot.

September 3, 1996—The 11th Reconnaissance Squadron becomes first Air Force unit to operate Predator, an unmanned aerial vehicle.

March 24, 1999—Operation Allied Force begins in Kosovo and the B-2 makes its operational debut.

1999

September 11, 2001—Terrorists strike the U.S. by hijacking commercial aircraft and flying them into buildings.

October 7, 2001—The first military strike in the war on terrorism begins with Operation Enduring Freedom.

March 19, 2003—Operation Iraqi Freedom begins.

December 15, 2005—The F-22 plane is declared operationally ready.

2003

Chapter Notes

Chapter One *A New Air Force Emerges*

1. "America Remembers," *CNN.com*, n.d., <http://www.cnn.com/SPECIALS/2002/america. remembers/sept11.section.html> (December 1, 2005).
2. The National Guard Association of the United States n.d., <http://www.ngaus.org/ngmagazine/main902. asp> (2005).
3. Ari Fleischer, *Taking Heat: The President, The Press and My Years in the White House* (New York: William Morrow, 2005), p. 141.
4. Ibid., p. 148.
5. Ibid., p. 150.

Chapter Two *History of American Aviation*

1. James L. Stokesbury, *A Short History of Air Power* (New York: William Morrow and Company, Inc., 1996), p. 13.
2. Herbert Molloy Mason, Jr., *The United States Air Force: A Turbulent History* (New York: Mason/Charter, 1976), p. 7.
3. Stokesbury, p. 14.
4. Ibid., p. 21.
5. James J. Hudson, *Hostile Skies: A Combat History of the American Air Service in World War I* (New York: Syracuse University Press, 1968), p. 3.
6. Ibid., pp. 4–5.
7. Mason, p. 67.
8. Ibid., p. 68.
9. Hudson, p. 139
10. Ibid., p. 186.
11. Ibid., p. 295.
12. Ibid., p. 299.
13. Mason, p. 74.

14. Ibid., p. 75.

15. Ibid., p. 76.

16. Ibid., p. 79.

17. Ibid., pp. 80, 82.

18. Ibid., p. 132.

19. Ibid., p. 141.

20. Edward Jablonski, *America in the Air War* (Alexandria, Va.: Time-Life Books, 1982), pp. 28, 30.

21. Kathleen T. Rhem, "Pentagon Hosts Salute to Hispanic World War II Veterans," *United States Department of Defense*, September 15, 2004, <http://www.defenselink. mil/news/Sep2004/n09152004_2004091513.html> (January 6, 2006).

22. Mason, p. 207.

Chapter Three   *The Air Force Is Born*

1. Herbert Molloy Mason, Jr., *The United States Air Force: A Turbulent History* (New York: Mason/Charter, 1976), p. 207.

2. Mason, p. 208.

3. Ivan Rendall, *Jet Combat From World War II to the Gulf War* (New York: The Free Press. 1997), p. 59.

4. James L. Stokesbury, *A Short History of Air Power* (New York: William Morrow and Company, Inc., 1996), p. 262.

5. "UN Offensive: September 16–November 2, 1950," *Air Force Historical Research Agency*, n.d., <http://www. au.af.mil/au/afhra/wwwroot/korean_war/ korean_ war_campaigns/un_offensive_091650_ 110250.html> (December 12, 2005).

6. "Korea, Summer 1953: May 1–July 27, 1953," *Air Force Historical Research Agency*, n.d., <http://www.au.af. mil/au/afhra/wwwroot/korean_war/korean_war_ campaigns/korea_summer_050153_072753.html> (December 12, 2005).

7. "The Korean War," *Korean War Veterans Memorial*,

July 11, 2002, <http://www.nps.gov/kwvm/war/
korea.htm> (December 1, 2005).

8. Stokesbury, p. 278.

9. Ibid., pp. 281–282.

10. Ibid., p. 284.

11. Benjamin S. Lambeth, "NATO'S Air War For Kosovo:
A Strategic and Operational Assessment," *Rand
Corporation, Project Air Force,* (Arlington, Va.: Rand),
p. 87.

12. Ibid.

13. John A. Tirpak, "Two Decades of Stealth," *Air Force
Magazine Online,* vol. 84, June 2001, <http://www.
afa.org/magazine/june2001/0601stealth. asp>
(January 1, 2006).

Chapter Four *The War on Terrorism*

1. George W. Bush, "Address to a Joint Session of Congress
and the American People," *The White House,* September
20, 2001, <http://www.whitehouse.gov/news/ releases/
2001/09/20010920-8.html> (January 1, 2006).

2. Jim Garamone, "America Launches Strikes Against Al
Qaeda, Taliban," *United States Department of Defense,*
October 7, 2001, <http://www.defenselink.mil/news/
Oct2001/n10072001_200110071.html> (January 1,
2006)

3. Matt Hasson, Lisa Polarek, and Gerry J. Gilmore,
"Striking from the Heartland," n.d., <http://www.
spear.navy.mil/profile/profile/dec01/pages/page18.
html> (January 6, 2006).

4. Linda D. Kozaryn, "Franks: Al Qaeda's Safe Harbor Is
Gone," *United States Department of Defense,* February
2, 2002, <http://www.defenselink.mil/news/Feb2002/
n02072002_200202072.html> (January 1, 2006).

5. "Final Results," *The 2004 Presidential Election,* n.d.,
<http://www.elections-afghanistan.org.af/Election%
20Results%20Website/english/enmain.htm>
(January 6, 2006).

6. George W. Bush, "President Says Saddam Hussein Must Leave Iraq Within 48 Hours," *The White House*, March 17, 2003, <http://www.whitehouse.gov/news/releases/2003/03/20030317-7.html> (January 1, 2006).

7. "White House fact sheet on Iraqi Freedom coalition partners," *The White House*, December 12, 2005, <http://www.whitehouse.gov/infocus/iraq/news/20030327-10.html> (January 2006).

Chapter Five   *The Air Force Today*

1. F. Whitten Peters and General Michael Ryan, "U.S. Air Force Expeditionary Aerospace Force press briefing," *U.S. Air Force*, August 4, 1998, <http://www.af.mil/lib/misc/eafbrief.html> (January 1, 2006).

2. John P. Jumper, "Resuming the AEF Battle Rhythm," *Air Force Policy Letter Digest*, June 2003, <http://www.af.mil/library/policy/letters/pl2003-06.html> (January 1, 2006).

3. "ARFC Facts and Figures," *Air Force Reserve Command*, August 22, 2005, <http://www.afrc.af.mil/FactSheets/facts_and_figures.htm> (January 1, 2006).

4. Ibid.

5. "Information About ESGR," *Employer Support for the Guard and Reserve*, n.d., <http://www.esgr.org/employers2/aboutESGR.asp?c=factUserra.html> (January 1, 2006).

6. "Operation Noble Eagle," *Air Force Link*, n.d., <http://www.af.mil/airforceoperationscenter/operationnobleeagle.asp> (January 1, 2006).

7. "Operation Joint Guardian," *Air Force Link*, n.d., <http://www.af.mil/airforceoperationscenter/operationjointguardian.asp> (January 1, 2006).

Chapter Six   *Structure of the Air Force*

1. "Air Combat Command," *Airman*, January 2005, <http://www.af.mil/news/airman/0105/acc.shtml> (December 12, 2005).

2. "Air Education and Training Command," *Airman*, January 2005, <http://www.af.mil/news/airman/0105/aetc.shtml> (December 12, 2005).

3. "Air Force Reserve Command," *Airman*, January 2005, <http://www.af.mil/news/airman/0105/afrc.shtml> (December 12, 2005).

4. "Air Force Special Operations Command," *Airman*, January 2005, <http://www.af.mil/news/airman/0105/afsoc.shtml> (December 12, 2005).

5. "Air Mobility Command," *Airman*, January 2005, <http://www.af.mil/news/airman/0105/amc.shtml> (December 12, 2005).

6. "Pacific Air Forces," *Airman*, January 2005, <http://www.af.mil/news/airman/0105/pacaf.shtml> (December 12, 2005).

7. "United States Air Forces in Europe," *Airman*, January 2005, <http://www.af.mil/news/airman/0105/usafe.shtml> (December 12, 2005).

8. "Air National Guard," *Airman*, January 2005, <http://www.af.mil/news/airman/0105/ang.shtml> (December 12, 2005).

Chapter Seven *Women and Minorities in the Air Force*

1. Air Force Instruction 36-2706, "Military Equal Opportunity (MEO) Program," *Air Force e-Publishing*, July 29, 2004, <http://www.e-publishing.af.mil/pubfiles/af/36/afi36-2706/afi36-2706.pdf> (January 1, 2006).

2. Valerie Moolman, *Women Aloft* (Alexandria, Va.: Time-Life Books, 1981), p. 9.

3. Ibid., p. 135.

4. Ibid., p. 139.

5. Ibid.

6. Ibid., pp. 135, 141.

7. Ibid., p. 149.

8. Ibid., p. 153.

9. "Highlights in the History of Military Women," *Women in Military Service for America Memorial*, n.d., <http://womensmemorial.org/Education/timeline.html> (January 1, 2006).

10. "Astronaut Bio: Eileen Collins," *National Aeronautics and Space Administration*, August 2005, <http://www.jsc.nasa.gov/Bios/html bios/collins.html> (January 9, 2006).

11. "Highlights in the History of Military Women."

12. Tuskegee Airmen, Inc., Organizational Website, <http://www.tuskegeeairmen.org/images/stats.pdf> (January 1, 2006).

13. Walter J. Boyne, "Question Mark," *Air Force Magazine Online*, vol. 86, March 2003, <http://www.afa.org/magazine/ march2003/0303qmark.asp> (January 1, 2006)

14. "Hispanic American Army Air Forces Heroes of World War II: Oscar Perdomo," *Air Education & Training Command*, <http://www.aetc.randolph.af.mil/ho/hispanic/his_perdomo.htm> (January 1, 2006).

15. "Review of Data on Hispanics 1993," *Defense Equal Opportunity Management Institute*, n.d., <https://www.patrick.af.mil/deomi/Observances%20&%20Demographics/Ethnic%20Observances/Hispanic%20Heritage%20Month/hhm93.htm> (January 2006).

16. "WW II Combat Europe Duty Above All: The Story of TSgt. Sator 'Sandy' Sanchez," *National Museum of the United States Air Force*, n.d., <http://www.wpafb.af.mil/museum/history/wwii/ce46.htm> (March 22, 2006).

17. Office of the Under Secretary of Defense (Personnel and Readiness), "Review of the Effectiveness of the Application and Enforcement of the Department's Policy on Homosexual Conduct in the Military," April 1998, <http://www.defenselink.mil/pubs/rpt040798.html> (January 9, 2006).

18. David F. Burrelli and Charles Dale, "Homosexuals and U.S. Military Policy: Current Issues," *Federation*

of American Scientists, May 27, 2005, <http://www.fas.org/sgp/crs/natsec/RL30113.pdf> (January 6, 2006).

19. "Interactive Demographic Analysis System (IDEAS)," *Air Force Personnel Center*, n.d., <https://www.afpc.randolph.af.mil/sasdemog/> (January 9, 2006).

Chapter Eight *Life on an Air Force Base*

1. Information taken from www.airforce.com and personal experiences

Chapter Nine *Joining the Air Force*

1. Lackland Air Force Base, Basic Military Training website, <http://www.lackland.af.mil/737web/bmt.htm> (December 12, 2005).

2. Bruce D. Callander, "Warrior Week," *Air Force Magazine Online*, volume 82, December 1999, <http://www.afa.org/magazine/Dec1999/1299warrior.asp> (January 1, 2006).

3. "U.S. Air Force Academy Overview," *United States Air Force Academy Public Affairs*, September 2002, <http://atlas.usafa.af.mil/pa/factsheets/overview.htm> (January 1, 2006).

4. "Academic Preparation," *Air Force Academy*, n.d., <http://academyadmissions.com/admissions/preparation/academic_prep.php> (January 1, 2006).

5. Robert F. Collins, *Reserve Officer Training Corps: Campus Paths to Service Commissions* (New York: Rosen Publishing Group, 1986), p. ix.

6. Ibid., p. 56.

7. Ibid., pp. 76–77.

8. "OTS Home Page," *Officer Training School*, <http://ots.afoats.af.mil/> (January 1, 2006).

Chapter Ten *Careers in the Air Force*

1. "Joint Specialized Undergraduate Pilot Training Fact Sheet," n.d., <http://www.af.mil/factsheets/factsheet.asp? fsID=181> (December 31, 2005).

2. "Our Mission," *Beale Air Force Base*, n.d., <http://www.beale.af.mil/7SWS/default.asp> (January 1, 2006).

3. "9th Munitions Squadron Mission," *Beale Air Force Base*, n.d., <http://www.beale.af.mil/9MUNS/default.asp> (January 1, 2006).

Chapter Eleven *Future of the Air Force*

1. John P. Jumper, "Speech to the 2005 Air Force Association Air Warfare Symposium," *The Air Force Association*, February 17, 2005, <http://www.afa.org/Media/scripts/Teets_Jumper_AWS05.asp#Jumper> (January 1, 2006).

2. Melanie Streeter, "Space integrates air forces to win wars," *Air Force Link*, February 17, 2004, <http://www.af.mil/news/story.asp?storyID=123006994> (January 1, 2006).

3. "527th Space Aggressor Squadron," *Peterson Air Force Base*, March 2004, <http://www.peterson.af.mil/hqafspc/Library/FactSheets/FactsSheets.asp?FactChoice=28> (January 1, 2006).

4. Richard J. Newman, "The Little Predator That Could," *Air Force Magazine Online*, vol. 85, March 2002, <http://www.afa.org/magazine/march2002/0302predator.asp> (January 1, 2006).

5. General John J. Jumper, "Shaping the Force," *Chief's Sight Picture*, January 29, 2004, <http://www.afpc.randolph.af.mil/retsep/Forceshaping/csafshapemsg.doc> (January 1, 2006).

Glossary

ace—Military pilot who shoots down more than five enemy aircraft.

Air Expeditionary Force (AEF)—Air Force combat and support forces are organized into ten AEFs to respond to recurring missions around the world.

Air Force One—The president's aircraft based at Andrews AFB.

air refueling—Aircraft receiving fuel from another aircraft in mid-flight.

base exchange (BX)—Shopping facility on most bases that resembles a department store.

Combat Air Patrols—Aerial fighting positions over a target or location.

court-martial—A military trial based on the Uniform Code of Military Justice.

deploy—To be sent overseas to support a military operation.

joint operation—A mission or exercise involving more than one military service.

mach—Equivalent to the speed of sound.

major command—The Air Force is organized into nine major commands.

military entrance processing station—Location where recruits are sent for physicals and testing prior to entering basic military training.

munitions—A weapon like a bomb or missile.

precision-guided munitions—Weapons guided to their targets by satellites or radar.

psychological operations—Using information against the enemy to destroy its morale or will to fight.

rank—A military designation that denotes an airman's status.

reconnaissance—Collecting information or intelligence on an enemy.

rules of engagement—Legal regulations in warfare.

squadron—Basic military unit made up of multiple flights.

sortie—One flight by an aircraft.

stealth—An airplane's ability to evade detection by radar.

UAV—Unmanned aerial vehicle.

ultimatum—A final warning or order.

Further Reading

Alagna, Magdalena. *Life Inside the Air Force Academy.* New York: Children's Press, 2002.

Atkins, Jeannine. *Wings and Rockets: The Story of Women in Air and Space.* New York: Farrar, Straus & Giroux, 2003.

Green, Michael and Gladys. *Long-range Bombers: The B-1B Lancers.* Mankato: Minn.: Capstone High-Interest Books, 2003.

———. *Night Attack Gunships: The AC-130H Spectres.* Mankato: Minn.: Capstone High-Interest Books, 2003.

———. *Remotely Piloted Aircraft: The Predators.* Mankato: Minn.: Capstone High-Interest Books, 2003.

———. *Stealth Attack Fighters: The F-117A Nighthawks.* Mankato: Minn.: Capstone High-Interest Books, 2003.

Hasday, Judy L. *The Tuskegee Airmen.* Philadelphia: Chelsea House Publishers, 2003.

Hopkins, Ellen. *The Thunderbirds: The U.S. Air Force Aerial Demonstration Squadron.* Mankato: Minn.: Capstone High-Interest Books, 2001.

———. *United States Air Force.* Chicago: Heinemann Library, 2004.

Langely, Wanda. *Flying Higher: The Women Airforce Service Pilots of World War II.* North Haven, Conn.: Linnet Books, 2002.

Roberts, Jeremy. *U.S. Air Force Special Operations.* Minneapolis: Lerner Publications, Co., 2005.

Santella, Andrew. *Air Force One.* The Millbrook Press, 2003.

Air Force Academy Admissions
<http://www.academyadmissions.com/>

Air Force Basic Military Training
<http://www.lackland.af.mil/737web/>

Air Force Web Site
<http://www.af.mil>

Index

A

Aerospace Expeditionary Forces (AEFs), 39–40, 103

Afghanistan, 32, 33–34, 42, 82, 94, 106

African Americans in the Air Force, 61–64

aircraft, 9–13, 14, 20, 25–26, 30, 35, 40, 41, 44, 46, 50, 52, 55, 57, 60, 65, 105–108

  Air Force One, 5, 6, 7

  bombers, 15, 17–19, 20, 22, 26, 30–31, 33–34, 35, 46, 57, 66, 107

  cargo, 7, 20, 36–37, 49

  fighters, 6–7, 17, 20, 22–23, 28, 31, 35, 38, 44, 46, 65, 67, 107–108

  reconnaissance/spy, 24, 30, 44, 46, 106

  stealth, 28, 30, 31, 33–34, 35, 46, 105–106

Air Education and Training Command (AETC), 46–47, 64

Air Force

  benefits, 71–73, 80, 83, 91–92

  careers, 93–102

  future, 103–109

  joining, 75–76, 83, 86–88

  medals, 82

  ranks, 81

  risks, 92

  structure, 45–50, 52–55

  training, 77–79, 84, 86, 88–91

Air Force Academy (USAFA), 84, 86

Air Force Agency for Modeling and Simulation, 53–54

Air Force bases (AFBs), 5, 6, 7, 31, 33, 37, 44, 45, 46, 47, 48, 49, 52, 53, 56, 58, 64, 66–67, 69–70, 71, 73–74, 77, 78, 79, 89, 90, 95, 98, 99, 100, 102, 103, 105, 108

Air Force Materiel Command (AFMC), 47–48

Air Force Reserve (AFR), 40–42, 44, 47, 49, 55, 101

Air Force Space Command (AFSPC), 49–50

Air Force Special Operations Command (AFSOC), 50

Air Mobility Command (AMC), 50, 52

Air National Guard (ANG), 41–42, 47, 54–55, 59

Al-Qaeda, 32–33, 34

Andrews Air Force Base, 5, 7, 64

Armed Services Vocational Aptitude Battery (ASVAB), 75–76

Army Air Force, 17, 18, 20, 21, 57, 61

Arnold, Hap, 57, 58

c.1